APPLE TV

Complete Users Guide With Tips And Tricks On How To Master Your Apple Tv (How Apple Tv App Works On Your iPhone, iPod, iTouch, Kodi, AirPods)

Sofie Lynge

Table of Contents

INTRODUCTION

Are you thinking of buying an Apple TV and looking for a book to read to gain the best knowledge as regards the Apple Tv? This book is well written and very helpful in setting up all the features of the new Apple TV system. All the explanations are easy to understand, and the writer doesn't bog you down with a lot of ultra-technical stuff that the average reader doesn't need in the first place.

This guide would take you through all the features of the Apple TV app to ensure that you take your entertainment game to the next level. Learn how to search for trending shows and movies, let Siri alert you when your favorite team has a game and lots more.

CHAPTER 1

What Is Apple TV? How Does It Work?

Despite the name, Apple Television isn't an actual television set. It's a streaming device similar to Roku and Amazon's Fire TV. The little black box is an inch-and-a-half tall, less than four inches along its sides, and runs on a platform similar to the iPhone and iPad, which means you can download a whole host of apps and games beyond standard streaming video from Netflix, Hulu, Amazon, etc.

What's Apple Tv?

Apple TV is designed for streaming movies and TV shows to your HDTV, much like Roku and Google's Chromecast, but that is only one feature. You can even listen to and watch podcasts on it, play games, stream music, and much more. It all depends on the applications you set up. Some programs are free, some cost money, and some are free to download but have something you have to buy to use it (e.g., HBO).

The only two things you will need to set up Apple TV (besides a certain TV) can be an HDMI cable (not included) and an internet connection. Apple Television consists of an Ethernet port for a hardwired Internet connection and also supports Wi-Fi. It also includes a remote control.

Once you hook it up to your Television via the HDMI wire and turn it on, you'll run through a short setup program. This process includes entering your Apple ID, which is the same ID you use to sign in to iTunes, and to download apps on your iPad. You will also need to type in your Wi-Fi information if you are connecting wirelessly.

The best part is if you have an iPhone, you can utilize it to speed up this process. Apple TV and the iPhone will share some of this information for you, avoiding the painful process of inputting data using a remote.

What Can Apple Television Do?

Illustration showing a woman using an Apple TV to watch a show on her television

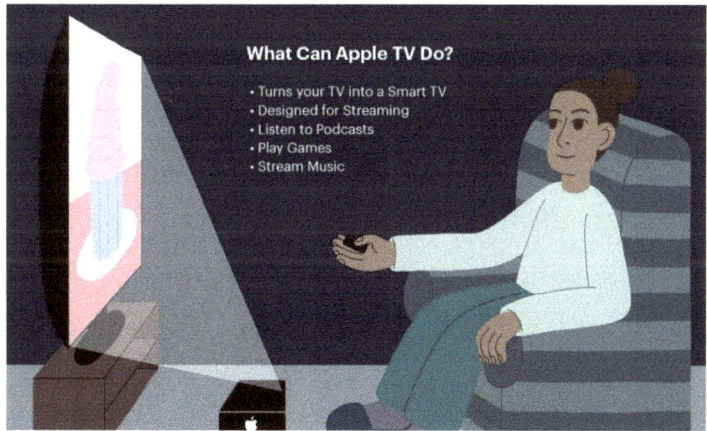

Apple TV turns your television into a "smart" Television. You can rent films or stream your collection from iTunes, stream movies and Television shows from applications like Netflix and Hulu Plus, stream music through Apple

Music and Pandora, listen to podcasts, and even use it to replace your traditional cable TV subscription with services like Sling TV.

Apple Television 4K has the same fast processor that powers the iPad Pro, which makes it as powerful as most laptop computers. Also, it has a fast graphics processor chip with enough power to transform it into a game console.

Apple Television is also hooked into the Apple ecosystem, which means it works great alongside your iPhone, iPad, and Mac. You can view your iCloud Photo Library on your TV, including those great "Memories" photo album videos the iPad and iPhone create automatically from your picture albums. You can also use AirPlay to throw your iPhone or iPad display screen to your Television, allowing you to interact with any app on your smartphone or tablet using your big screen tv.

Does Apple TV Work with HomeKit?

Apple Television also gives you access to Siri and can become a base station for Home Kit. The remote control includes a Siri button, letting you control your TV by voice. You can even utilize the Siri-like functionality for requests such as telling you the actors in a specific movie or asking it to display all Matt Damon films.

Home Kit is the headquarters for your smart home. When you have smart appliances like a thermostat or lights, you can use Home Kit to control them. You can even use your iPhone away from home to communicate with Apple TV in your home to regulate your smart devices.

What Are the Differences Between the Apple Television Models?

There are currently two different models for sale, and one model recently discontinued. And as you can expect, there are some significant differences between them.

Apple TV 4K. This is the flagship of the Apple Television model. It facilitates 4K and HDR video and is powered by the same A10 processor found in the iPad Pro. If you're looking to buy Apple Tv, this is the top-shelf model.

Apple TV (4th Generation). This model supports 1080p HD video and is run by the A8 processor chip, which is the same processor in the iPhone 6. While you may be tempted to buy the 4th-generation if you don't have a television that facilitates 4K or HDR, this model not only buys you the ability to upgrade your TV in the future, it also doubles the speed of the processor chip and quadruples the velocity of the graphics.

Apple Television (3rd Era). This model is no more on the market by Apple, but you may find one at auction sites like eBay or person-to-person sites like Craigslist. This version delivers video streaming capabilities without the processing power; this means it doesn't have access to the application store. It's cheaper than the other models because it's old, but you might be better off investing in another streaming device just like a Roku or Amazon Open fire TV.

What Is Apple Tv 4K?

While priced higher than all of its competitors, Apple Television 4K may end up being the best bargain in loading devices. Apple TV 4K is great for several reasons, the best of which being that if you own one, Apple will upgrade your iTunes movie collection to 4K.

The average cost difference between an HD version of a movie and a 4K version of the movie is around $5-$10. This means if you have ten videos in your iTunes movie library, you are getting around a $75 value in the upgrade to 4K alone. If you have twenty-five films, Apple Television 4K practically pays for itself.

Unless you already own a movie, Apple will let you pick up the 4K version for the same price as the HD. You won't have to pay a premium to get the same movie in its best format.

In terms of picture quality, Apple TV 4K supports both 4K resolution and HDR10. While 4K has all the buzz, High Dynamic Range (HDR) may be more important to display quality. As Apple puts it, 4K provides you more pixels on your screen, while HDR gives you better pixels. Instead of just increasing the quality, HDR gives you a higher range of colors to improve the quality and depth of the image. Apple Television 4K also facilitates Dolby Vision, which is a form of HDR with a higher color range.

But Apple TV isn't just about streaming video. The processor in the Apple TV 4K is the same as the A10X Fusion processor chip in the second-generation iPad Pro. The apparent beneficiary here is gaming, but it has so much control power that you might start seeing productivity apps like Numbers and Pages come to the Apple Television.

Apple TV 4K also shines with internet connectivity. Not only does it include a 1 Gigabit Ethernet slot, but it also gets the latest Wi-Fi technology, including MIMO, which stands for multiple-in-multiple-out. When you have a dual-band router, Apple Television 4K essentially connects to it twice (once on each "band"). The doubled-up wireless connection can be faster than a single wired one, and it is helpful when dealing with 4K content.

What's the Apple Tv App?

Since we live in a world of streaming where lots of things

are available at any time, it can be a bit paralyzing to figure out what to watch. And thanks to so many different services, where you can watch it.

Apple's answer is a new app, simply called "Television." In many ways, it is the same as what you get when you open Hulu Plus or other similar apps. You'll see a variety of different shows and movies, starting with those you've lately watched and expanding to suggested titles. The big difference is that these videos are coming from a variety of sources, like Hulu Plus, HBO Now, as well as your movie collection in iTunes. The TV app gathers all of this content in one place so you can easily browse through all of it. It even has a Sports channel that will show live events, including the current scores. Unfortunately, Netflix is not integrated into Apple's TV app, so you'll still need to check that app independently.

What Platforms Will the Apple Television App Focus On?

The Apple Television app - and for that reason Apple TV Stations and Apple Television+ (if they are released) -

functions on the following devices and systems:

- iOS gadgets (iPhone, iPad, iPod iTouch).

- Apple TV

- Macs.

- Amazon Fire Television devices.

- Roku devices.

- Wise TVs from LG, Samsung, Sony, and Vizio.

At this time, the Apple Television app is on iOS products and the Apple Television hardware. The application will be accessible in over 100 countries on the additional devices in-May 2019.

Isn't Apple Television A Hardware Package?

It is! That's where Apple is using the name "Apple Television" to refer to a lot of things so as not to get people to confuse. Not only is it an app, but Apple TV can also be a hardware gadget utilized for entertainment.

Apple has offered gadgets called Apple Television since 2007. While it's evolved through the years, the latest edition - the Apple Television 4K, released in 2017 - is a robust entertainment gadget. It runs all types of apps, including streaming video apps, video games designed particularly for the Apple Television, Apple Music, and even more. Apple Television also regulates smart-home products as a Home-kit hub.

The Apple Television application comes pre-set up on the Apple Television hardware. Because the Apple TV application works on multiple gadgets, the Apple Television 4K doesn't need to make use of the Apple Television app, Apple Television Stations, or Apple Television+.

CHAPTER 2

Apple TV User Guide

Apple TV is a streaming media box that shows movies, TV shows, music, and live events to you through your television. If you're new to Apple Television, then you need this Apple TV user guide to help you master all the ins and outs and get the most out of your original streaming box.

NOTE: This guide supports tv-OS versions 13, 12, 11, 10, 9, 8, 7, and 6 - 4th, 3rd, and 2nd generation Apple TVs. This guide also covers iTunes and Apple Television app on macOS variations Catalina (10.15) - Mountain Lion (10.8).

How Do I Set up Apple TV?

If you have just purchased an Apple TV, then zip on over to the Apple Television setup guide. Be sure to sign in to your iCloud account on the device and connect to your

Wi-Fi. Now you're ready to start using it.

How to Operate Apple TV?

Apple excels at creating beautiful interfaces, and Apple Television is no exception. The home screen displays a sampling of content, and below it is several menus using large rounded icons for each channel or function. The simple remote allows you to breeze left and right, up and down between each image, and select the center button or touch area.

The first row of icons contains category symbols for Movies, TV Shows, and Music. There is also an icon that shows your connected Computers and then one for Settings. On Apple Television 4th generations, you will also see an App Store icon.

Just below that, you will see all your favorite channels like Netflix, Hulu, and even one for playing Apple live occasions.

Notice: To rearrange the apps on your home display, use the Siri remote to select an app, then press until it starts to shake. Then, using the touchpad, move it to the new location and press the touchpad again to save it.

The Apple TV Remote

Let's touch on a few Apple Television basics. Depending on the Apple TV package version you have, your Apple TV remote may have directional buttons (silver remote control for 2nd and 3rd generations). When you have a newer Apple Television (4th era), then you will have a touchpad to navigate.

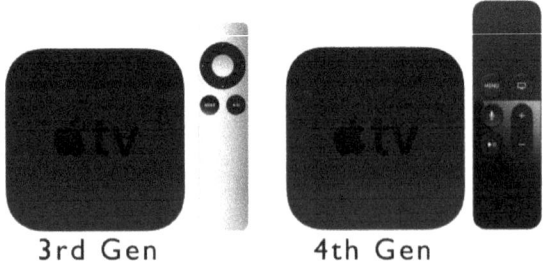

3rd Gen   4th Gen

On the newer remote, swipe along the left and right to get around through the selections and icons and tap the touchpad to choose. On the older remote control, use the directional control keys to move between symbols and the guts button to select.

All remotes have a menu button and a pause/play button. The newer remotes have a home button, along with controls to turn the volume up and down. On the old (silver) remote, the menu button works as a "back" button that takes you one level back throughout the system.

The newer versions (HD and 4K) have Siri built-in so you can use voice commands to search for Television shows and films, play content, open apps, and more. You can even use your iPhone as an Apple TV remote by downloading the corresponding application to your phone.

Some voice commands to try are:

- "Open Netflix."

- "Play the latest episode of South Park."

- "What football games are on?"

- "Play some jazz music."

To use the Siri function, hold down the microphone button for a couple of seconds, then say your command when you hear a beep.

Searching on an Apple TV

Searching on an older Apple TV is different from using an Apple Television with Siri. With the earlier decades (2nd and 3rd), you must first select the category of Movies, TV, or Music, then scroll over on the top menu to choose Search. You will see a keyboard and can choose letters, numbers, and symbols to type in the name of the movie or show you're looking for, then choose from the results.

NOTE: As soon as you begin typing, results will display for you to choose from. You won't have to put in the entire name of your favorite movie or TV show.

To search on the Siri-enabled remote, press the Siri button and keep hold until you hear a beep. Speak your request into the remote control to search, and Siri will deliver. Siri also searches within applications like Netflix, Hulu, and HBO to find precisely what you need.

Apple Television Apps and Content

The best thing about a loading device is access to hundreds of stations and apps. One of the most popular uses for an Apple TV is to play games. With a more recent version of Apple TV, you have access to thousands of apps through the App Store. Follow the instructions below to find and install games and applications on your Apple Television.

- From the home screen, choose the App Store icon.

- Use either the Featured selection or Siri to find the game or app you want.

- Select the application icon to install it. Some apps require a purchase, and some are free.

- The app will now appear on your home display screen prepared to use.

Stream Films to Apple TV from Your Mac

Although you can download the official Apple Television manually online and find out how to watch movies from your Mac, this is a quicker and easier method. If you like to rent DVDs, then rip them to your computer, you can create your home library of films and watch them through your Apple TV device. Using this same method, you can also share photos, music, and TV shows.

Add Movies On Your Mac

Once you rip the DVDs to your personal computer, you can store them in any folder. Then follow the steps below to get the TV App or iTunes (for older operating systems) to recognize your movies.

USING ITUNES

To get iTunes to identify your movies, follow these steps:

- Open iTunes.

- Navigate to Movies.

- Go to File > Add to Library.

- Browse for the folder or file you want to add.

- Press the Open button, and iTunes will add these to your library.

- The movies are now shared and ready to view on Apple TV.

Using the apple television app on the mac (macOS Catalina)

To get the Apple TV application on the Mac pc to recognize your films, follow these steps:

- Open TV on the Macintosh.

- Click Library at the top.

- Click Document > Import.

- Choose a folder of movies or a file.

- Your videos are now shared and prepared to watch on your Apple Television.

Turn On Home Sharing

You will need to turn on Home Sharing for everything to

work together nicely. The process is slightly different for old variations of macOS before Catalina.

- **For iTunes (macOS Mountain Lion - Mojave):** Open up iTunes and go to File > Home Posting, then enter your Apple ID and password when prompted.

- **For Apple TV on Mac (macOS Catalina):** Open Systems Preferences and click the Writing icon. Then, in the left-hand pane, click Media Sharing and check off Home Posting. You can also give your library a name in the container above.

Log Into Your Apple Television To Watch The Movies

After setting up your Apple TV and logging in with your Apple ID and security password, you will now have access to use those films, photos, and music. On the home screen of Apple Television, select the Computer systems icon. You will notice categories of your shared music, Television shows, movies, and photos. Scroll through to find the video you want and hit select to start playing it.

Apple TV App vs. Apple Television Box

Now that Apple has released its Apple TV app on other devices, the media box may someday face extinction. For now, however, Apple Television is alive and offers one of the best interfaces, high-quality content streaming, and seamless integration with Home Kit and iCloud services.

The Apple Television app, which can be used on any iOS device and other devices, offers some of the same content and features of the package. However, it does not come with a remote or the ability to share screens via AirPlay or stream your libraries. Along with the Apple TV app, Apple has rolled out its own set of proprietary content, and TV shows that you cannot view anywhere else.

CHAPTER 3

What Is Apple Tv+, and How Does It Work?

After years of speculation and a star-studded preview event, Apple Tv+ is finally here. But Apple Tv+ brings a lot of questions along with it. Read on to learn the answers to all of your questions about Apple's streaming video service.

What's Apple Tv+?

Apple Tv+ is Apple's loading TV and movie platform. Think of it as Apple's answer to Netflix, Hulu, or Disney+. It's a service that you subscribe which gives you access to original content available only on Apple Tv+.

Apple Tv+ Is Different from the Apple Television App

This is a bit confusing since they have very similar names, but Apple TV+ is not the same thing as the Apple Television app. The Apple TV+ service can be used within the Apple Television app, but the app provides many other features and options.

The Apple TV app is a place to watch content from many different services that you sign up to. For instance, if you subscribe to Netflix, Hulu, and Showtime, the Apple Television application shows the latest episodes of your favorite shows from all of those services, plus recommendations for other things you may enjoy. It also offers content from the iTunes Store and lets you buy and rent movies there. You can use it without subscribing to Apple Television+.

Apple TV+, on the other hand, is one source of content (Apple's content) that can be accessed from the Apple Television app.

Apple TV+ Is Also Different From Apple Television

Channels

Apple TV Channels is a feature of the Apple TV app that enables you to subscribe to streaming services through the Apple Television app. Services available via Channels include things like HBO, Showtime, and CBS All Access. You can sign up for Stations through the Apple TV app using your Apple ID. You can use Channels without signing up to Apple Television+, or in addition to it.

Apple TV+ Requires No Special Hardware to Use

Apple's set-up loading device called the Apple TV is undoubtedly one way to access the Apple Tv+ streaming service (and the Apple TV app, and Apple Television Channels), but it's not the only option.

Apple TV+ is available on a wide range of devices, including:

- iOS devices (iPhone and iPod touch)

- iPad-OS devices

- Apple TV

- Macs

- Amazon Fire Television devices

- Roku devices

- Smart Televisions from LG, Samsung, Sony, and Vizio

Content Available on Apple Television+

At launch, Apple TV+ offers a library of Television series and films, including

Apple Tv+ Television Series

- Dickinson, a series focusing on the young life of poet Emily Dickinson.

- For All Mankind, a science fiction series from Battlestar Galactica creator.

- Ghostwriter, a continuation of the children's series.

- Helpsters, another children's series in which monsters solve problems.

- The Morning Show, starring Jennifer Aniston, Reese Witherspoon, and Steve Carell

- An Oprah Winfrey series of conversations with authors.

- See, a string about a world where humans have lost the capability to see, starring Jason Momoa and Alfre Woodard.

- Snoopy in Space, Peanuts animated show.

Apple Tv+ Movies

- The Elephant Queen, a documentary about elephant extinction.

Other shows and movies set to be released at later dates include:

- Astounding Stories, a fantasy anthology series produced by Steven Spielberg

- Foundation, adapting Isaac Asimov's group of science fiction novels

- Lisey's Story, adapting the Stephen King novel, made by J.J. Abrams and starring Julianne Moore

- On the Rocks, written and directed by Sophia Coppola, starring Bill Murray and Rashida Jones.

- Untitled new Peanuts series

- Various Sesame Workshop series.

- An untitled documentary produced by Oprah Winfrey.

- A full list of all announced programming for Apple Tv+ can be found on Wikipedia.

Many loading services release all shows of their TV series at the same time to let users binge-watch the whole series. Apple Television+ takes a different approach to release new episodes.

For most TV series, the first three shows will be released in a group. After that, new episodes will be issued once a week. That schedule may change for some series, which will be released all at once for binging, but most will work that way.

Note: New series will debut each month, according to Apple.

Does Apple Television+ Offer a Deep Library of Content

like Netflix?

No. Apple TV+ requires a very different method of content than Netflix, Hulu, and Disney+. Those services have vast libraries of Television series and movies, mixing new releases with extensive selections of content released in the past. Apple TV+ only offers materials created for (or acquired for release on) Apple Television+.

This means that the collection of content on Apple TV+ at launch is much smaller than other services. The library will grow over time as Apple launches new shows and films, and as it acquires other materials.

Can You Watch Apple Television+ Offline?

Yes. As long as your subscription is valid, you can download Apple TV+ content to mobile devices to watch even when you're not connected to the internet.

Apple Television+ Subscriptions and Free Trials

Apple TV+ costs US$4.99/month for a family

membership. Apple Television+ also has a free trial. You can try it out for seven days before you have to subscribe or cancel.

The standard Apple TV+ subscription facilitates up to 6 users in a Family Writing group. No specific price has been announced (although $4.99 is a reasonable guess), and Apple hasn't said whether plans for more users would be available, but that seems unlikely since Family Sharing has a 6-consumer maximum.

Also, if you buy a new iPhone, iPad, iPod iTouch, Apple Television, or Mac, you'll get one free year of Apple TV+ included with your device. From then on free first 12 months, you'll have to either continue the subscription or cancel. You have 90 days after purchase to activate the free membership.

How to Subscribe to Apple Television+

You'll need the Apple TV app running on a compatible device and an Apple ID with a credit card on file. If you have those things, just go to the Apple Television app, find the Apple TV+ content, and follow the onscreen prompts.

The monthly cost of Apple Television+ will be billed to

your on-file credit card, just like any other services you've subscribed to through your Apple devices.

Apple TV+ Availability

Apple Television+ is available in the U.S. and over 100 other countries and regions on Nov 1, 2019.

CHAPTER 4

How to Use the Apple TV Remote App

Apple Television is the gateway to streaming content, not to mention your movies, music, and photos. The remote is sleek and small and very easy to lose. As a backup option, Apple TV owners can download the free Apple Television Remote App to make sure that they're never without a remote when they need one.

Take note: The Apple TV Remote App needs to be paired with your Apple Tv(s), which requires the Apple TV Remote. So, it's a good idea to download the app and pair your Apple Television when you first set it up, before your remote gets lost or runs out of battery.

If you're using iOS 12 or other iOS series, the Apple TV Remote is automatically added to the Control Center. This version will continue to work with Apple Television 4th generation or Apple TV 4K. If you are hanging on to a mature device (Apple Television or iPhone), you can download the Remote-control App in the App Store for free and manually add your device(s).

Preparing to Use Apple TV Remote App

Before pairing your Apple Television with the Remote App, make sure that both your Apple TV and your mobile device are running the most current version of their own software.

NOTE: For you to be able to arranged your Apple Television to automatically set up new updates when they are available. For Apple TV 4K or 4th era go to Configurations > System > Software Updates and start Automatic Update. To update the software automatically on Apple Television 2nd or 3rd generation, go to Settings > General > Upgrade Software and turn on Update Automatically.

Using the Apple TV App with iPhone, iPad, or iPod Touch

You can download the Apple Television Remote application from the App Store on your iPhone, iPad, or iPod touch. Then you're ready to set up your Apple TV to work with your device.

- Make sure that your Apple Television as well as your device using the Remote control app are linked to the same Wi-Fi network.

- Utilize the Apple TV Remote to turn on your Apple TV.

- Open the Remote-control App on your device, then touch Add Apple Tv.

Tap the name of the Apple TV that you would like to add to your Remote App. Apple TVs on your network will appear by name, which was assigned at setup. We recommend naming Apple Televisions based on their location in your home, such as Family Room or Master Bedroom, for easy access when using the Remote App.

Your Apple Television will now screen a four-digit code on your tv, which you'll enter into the display that automatically appears on your iPhone, iPad, or iPod iTouch.

Using the Apple TV Remote App

Given that your Apple TV is linked to your mobile device you're prepared to use the Remote-control App to control and access your Apple Television content.

- Launch the Remote App.

- Select the Apple TV that you wish to control from the iTunes Remote display screen.

- Touch or scroll on your touch screen to navigate your content and use the Menu and Play/Pause buttons.

- Tap the ? (question mark) at the very top right for help using the navigation screen.

- Touch Done in the top right corner to gain access to the More menu and navigate your iTunes content.

At the menu you can pick from shortcuts at the bottom to access your Playlists, Artists, Albums or return to the Control touchscreen of the app.

Using the black Control screen is essentially the same as using the latest Apple Television Remotes that come with the 4K version. The Remote-control App is an upgrade from older Apple TV remotes, allowing quicker scrolling and easier navigation.

Benefits of the Apple Television Remote App

The remote that comes with an Apple Tv is, as most Apple products are, smooth and attractive. It is also very prone to sliding between couch cushions or being misplaced due to its small size. Having the Remote App on at least one Apple device means that when your normal remote control is missing, you'll still have a way to use your Apple TV.

Older Apple Television remotes use small button batteries, which are easily replaced but not something most people keep on hand. A dead remote control means no Apple TV, so owners of old versions can really benefit from the app. The Remote-control App also doesn't require line-of-sight visibility to your Apple Television box, which older Apple TV remotes need. This is great if your media is stored in a cabinet or behind your Television. It's also super handy for parents to be able to pause or start a show for their kids from another room.

The Remote App has one more huge benefit over the remotes that include your Apple TV: when you need to enter text, the app provides a keyboard. No more scrolling across to select letters one at a time when you're trying to sign into a streaming app!

CHAPTER 5

The Latest Apple Tv 6 Rumors

There's a lot of interest in what the 6th era Apple TV box is going to offer to it's users. And with good reason! Our new golden age of television is being driven in part by Netflix, Amazon, and Apple (along with plenty of others) pouring billions into new and award-winning shows. Most of these shows are only available via loading and you will need to get a device from Roku, Amazon, Google, or Apple to enjoy them.

The most recent new Apple TV model was the Apple Tv 4K, released in Sept. 2017, which means it's just about time for a fresh model (or models!) to debut. While Apple has yet to announced the Apple TV 6, the rumor mill is churning with ideas about what it will offer and when we'll be able to get our hands on one.

What To Expect from the 6th Generation Apple

Television (2020)

- Multiple models and form factors
- Siri improvements
- A revised remote control
- Improved internal hardware
- Integrated Apple loading video service
- Lower prices.

More Information on the Next-Generation Apple TV

Rumors

While these features and offerings are all still rumors and conjecture until Apple makes an official announcement, the 6th generation Apple Television device may include the following features.

Multiple Models and Form Factors

While Apple offers a single Apple TV model - a

hockey-puck-sized dark square - other streaming device makers have a much wider variety of options. From boxes to dongles like the Chromecast to tiny sticks that plug into Television USB ports like the Amazon Fire TV and the Roku Streaming Stick, there are a lot of options out there (and a lot of price points, too). Given the popularity of the smaller devices, and Apple's need to sell more hardware to set with its streaming video service (more on that later), expect the next-generation Apple Television to come in a number of shapes, sizes, and prices.

Improved Siri Features

The 4th Era Apple Tv and Apple Tv 4K already support Siri – this will greatly be of help to search for films and Television shows by tone of voice - but expect the Apple Tv 6 to do a lot more with Siri. Apple's Home Pod smart speaker provides a good idea of what improved Siri features in an Apple Television might look like. Forget speaking into the handy remote control to use Siri as you do now. The next-generation Apple TV could allow you to simply talk out loud and have the set-up container hear and respond to you. We could also see support for Siri via the wireless Air Pod earbuds delivered with this model.

Revised Remote

The Siri Remote control that is included with the Apple TV is one of the device's most controversial features. Many people find it slippery, hard to figure out, and just plain too small. It's a pretty solid bet that the 2020 Apple Television will include a revised remote control. Modifications to its form factor are likely, some other interesting gossips for the remote include the Touch ID fingerprint scanner integrated into the remote for use in authorizing purchases, logging into accounts, and for security.

Improved Internals: Faster Performance and More Storage

The Apple TV 4K is snappy in terms of performance, whether you're loading video or playing games. Apple has made big strides in the performance of the A-series processors used in the iPhone and iPad since the Apple TV was released, and that means you should expect the Apple Television 6 to benefit from those chips. A speedier processor will come in most useful with games, where the Apple TV will deliver performance that begins to rival some dedicated gaming consoles.

While not a major upgrade, storage-capacity increases are common with new years of Apple products. The Apple Television 4K offers 32GB and 64GB of storage, which is the same storage space that the previous generation had, too. As games and applications become ever-more-hungry for storage, expect the Apple TV 6 to offer something like 64GB and 128GB (or more) of storage space.

Apple Loading Video Service

Apple's streaming video service won't be exclusive to the 6th Generation Apple Television, but it will be a big selling point for these devices. As Apple increasingly focuses on selling services and not just hardware, a monthly subscription-based loading video offering will be a big element of that strategy.

Lower Price

The Apple TV 4K is relatively expensive, operating US$179-$199, while competing devices from Amazon, Google, and Roku cost as little as US$35. Since Apple seems to be particularly interested in offering subscriptions to its streaming video service, it's easy to imagine Apple Television price cuts being used to tempt subscribers. If the 6th Era Apple TV does deliver multiple shapes and sizes, expect that some of those models will start at $100.

Unlikely, But Interesting, Rumors

There are always some rumors floating around that are improbable to happen (and least with this model) but still worth thinking about. Some far-fetched, but interesting, rumors about the 2020 Apple TV include:

Face ID: Some gossips suggest that Apple could bring its Face ID facial recognition technology to the Apple Television. It would be used for unlocking the device, authorizing purchases, loading personalized settings, and more. That is less likely since it would require the addition of a camera to the Apple TV hardware and that wouldn't work with smaller form factors.

The end of the Apple Television: Apple made big news early in 2019 when it announced a series of deals to integrate iTunes, AirPlay, Home kit, and other key technologies in TVs made by Samsung, LG, Sony, and others. While this was seen generally as a step preparing for the release of the loading video service, it could also be the first step to the end of the Apple TV. After all, if you can get all of Apple's video systems built into your Television, why buy the hardware? It seems unlikely that Apple would make such a radical move right now, but it isn't impossible.

CHAPTER 6

15 Awesome Things You Can Do With Apple TV

You may think you know what you can do with the Apple Television, but if your idea of the benefits of the Apple Television is mostly streaming video and audio, and maybe a little gaming, you're selling the device short. Apple TV is fully packed of awesome, hidden features. Here are 15 of the best things you probably didn't know you are able to do with the Apple TV.

01 Find Free Streaming Options

Apple Tv's universal search feature

When you're looking for something to view, don't search inside apps. If you use the Apple Tv's common voice search, it checks every app you have installed to let you know your options. It might even find a way to watch the show or movie that you didn't know about free of charge.

To find content this way, hold down the Siri button on the remote control and say "Show me [the name of the thing you're looking for]." Select your item in the results that pop up at the bottom of the display. Around the search result display screen, look for the Available Online beneath the description for your options. Click Open In to start the video in your preferred app.

02 Don't Miss Hard to Hear Dialogue

Using the Apple Television, you never have to miss mumbled or otherwise hard-to-hear dialogue. If you miss what one character says to another, keep down the Siri button on the Siri Remote control and say "what did he/she say?" The video will skip back a few seconds, temporarily start closed captioning, and boost the volume.

03 Fast Forward or Go Back Precisely with Siri

Want to miss ahead in a movie or Television show exactly 102 mere seconds or go back 8 minutes? You can do it using Siri and the Apple TV. Just hold down the Siri button on the Siri Handy remote control and tell Apple

TV what you want: "return back 2 minutes," "skip forward 90 secs," etc.

04 Gain access to Subtitles and Audio Settings

A lot of the content available on Apple Television has optional subtitles available. To access them, start watching any video and swipe down on the Siri Remote. Select Subtitles and then swipe across to the language you want. Click the remote to carefully turn on subtitles in that language.

Hint: Subtitles aren't the only options you can gain access to this way. If you select Sound, you can control the spoken vocabulary of the video you're viewing. You can even access audio configurations like equalizing volume to reduce loud sounds, and chose the speakers the audio is being sent to, including Home Pods.

05 Control Your HDTV With Apple TV Remote

Forget the need of multiple remotes to regulate different parts of your Tv setup. When you have an Apple Television, you can use its Siri Remote control to power parts of your TV. With all the right settings enabled, the

Siri Remote control can turn on your TV, receiver, and Apple Television at the same time, as well as control the volume on your TV.

To do this, go to Configurations > General > Remotes and Devices. First, toggle the Control TVs and Receivers menu to On. Then click Volume Control and choose the option you prefer.

06 Display Your iPhone, iPad, or Mac pc on Your TV

With Apple Television you can project your iPhone, iPad, or Macintosh onto your High definition tv. This feature is great for viewing photos on a large screen, playing videos from your device, or giving a presentation. To get this done, you need to use Air Play Mirroring, an attribute included in iOS, macOS, and tv OS.

07 Use Dark Mode at Night

The Apple TV's interface is filled with big, bright, appealing colors and images. But that isn't necessarily the best if you're watching in the dark. In that case, you might prefer a more muted look. You can get it with the Apple Tv's Dark Setting. Enable this and the design of the home display gets darker and more appropriate for low-light viewing.

To enable Apple TV Dark Mode, click Settings >Appearance > Dark.

08 Use Apple Television to Control Your Smart Home

To automate your home with internet-connected smart home devices like thermostats, lights, and cameras, you need a smart home hub. The hub helps devices to communicate with each other and lets you control them over the internet. For smart-home devices that use Apple's Home kit standard, you don't need a separate device - your Apple TV can play this role for you.

To allow your Apple TV's smart home features, go to Settings > Accounts > iCloud > toggle My Home to Connected.

09 Pair Bluetooth Headphones, Game Controllers, and Keyboards

Apple TV supports all kinds of Bluetooth accessories, including keyboards, cellular headphones, and game controllers. If you have a Bluetooth accessory, you can connect it to your Apple Television. Put the item in pairing mode and then go to Settings > Remotes and Devices > Bluetooth and select the accessory you want to pair. If these devices require a pin to set, enter it.

10 Use iPhone, iPad, or Apple Watch as Remote Control

In the event that you lose the Siri Handy remote control or just don't choose it, you may use your iPhone, iPad, or even your Apple Watch as a remote. For the iPad and Apple Watch, you'll need Apple's free Remote application (for the Watch, Remote control must be installed on the iPhone the Watch is matched to). When you have an iPhone working iOS 11 and up, Apple TV controls are built right into Control Center.

11 Use Any Handy Remote Control, Not Just The Siri Remote

If your Apple Television is part of a home theater system, you certainly need a universal remote that controls all of your components. With the remote you will be able to use it to control the Apple TV instead of relying on the Siri Remote or the app. You'll need to help the Apple Television "learn" the options, features, and control keys of your general remote.

12 Launch Screensavers Using the Remote

The Apple Tv's gorgeous, hypnotic screensavers pop-up after a few minutes of the TV sitting idle, but you can force them to launch immediately using the Siri Remote control. To do this, go directly to the Apple TV home display screen and move to the top still left corner of the screen. Then press the Menu button on the remote.

NOTE: Pressing the Menu button while on the Home display will move you to the upper-left part automatically.

13 Make Apple Television a Business Tool with Conference Room Display

Apple TV makes a great addition to offices. Because AirPlay enables you to project a computer or device onto it, the Apple Television makes it easy to give presentations on the big screen. When you put the Apple

TV in Meeting Room Display setting, the TV is available for anyone to hook up to and use. With that mode, the TV shows a screensaver and instructions on how to connect.

To enable this, go to Configurations > AirPlay > Conference Room Screen and toggle Meeting Room Display to On.

14 Reboot Using the Remote Control

Just like an iPhone or computer, you need to reboot the Apple Television sometimes to solve problems. An option in the Settings app will do this, nevertheless, you can save a bunch of clicks by rebooting using the Siri Remote control. To do that, hold down the home and Menu buttons on the remote control at the same time until the light on the front of the Apple TV begins to blink. Then let go of the control keys, and the Apple Television will restart.

15 Keep Multiple Apple Televisions in Sync

If you own more than one Apple TV, you probably want

them to have the same group of apps and options. You don't have to arrange or sync them by hand, however. With the One Home Screen feature, you don't have to worry about it. Enable this option, and all Apple TVs using the same iCloud accounts automatically stay in sync for the applications they have installed, how the apps are arranged, folders, and more.

To allow One Home Display, go to Settings > Accounts > iCloud and toggle One Home Display screen to On.

CHAPTER 7

How to Get Plex on Your Apple Tv

Plex is a program that runs on many devices and operating system that allows for video sharing. The application streams video content across multiple devices.

Once you set up Plex on your computer and have your computer attached to your media library, and soon you'll be able to access your videos, music, and even photos from anywhere. Plex is programmed at playing content on local network devices, like smart Television boxes like the Apple TV.

Plex works best on the fourth generation of Apple Television, but with a little blood, sweat, and tears (okay just a little nerdery), you can get Plex working on a third-generation Apple TV.

Identifying Your Apple Television Model

Third-generation Apple Tv's and the earlier ones do not

63

ship with the Plex app, and additional apps cannot be installed on the device. However, those willing to do a little software hacking should be able to get Plex to run on their older Apple TV series. We can use the Plex Connect workaround to perform Plex on a third-generation Apple TV, but it is just a little challenging to get it running.

If you have a fourth-generation or newer version of Apple Television, you can use the tv-OS App Store to download the Plex app for Apple TV.

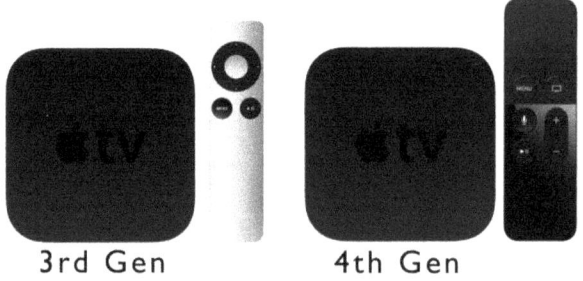

3rd Gen   4th Gen

It's not easy to tell the difference between the two Apple TVs at a glance. Both are small black boxes with rounded edges. The fourth-generation Apple Television comes with the dark touch-sensitive Siri remote and was released in 2015. The third-generation Apple TV comes with a silver remote control with a control wheel and premiered in 2012.

If you're having a hard time sorting out which is which, use Apple's guide to identifying your Apple Television.

Installing Plex on the Fourth-Generation Apple TV or

Later

When compared with the procedure for installing Plex on a third-generation Apple Television, the process for a fourth-generation and later Apple TV is comically simple.

- Open the App Store application on your Apple TV. Search for the Plex app and download it to your Apple Television.

- Open up the Plex app. Follow the instructions on the screen to connect to your Plex account using the provided link and four-digit code.

- Select your Plex server from the list and start streaming content.

Installing Plex on the Third-Generation Apple TV

The installation procedure for the third-generation Apple Television is far from simple. Read the installation process from start to the end before beginning to gauge your comfort level with each step.

It requires configuring your host device (PC or Mac), your network, and your Apple TV. We'll be using Python scripts to duplicate an existing Apple TV application then trick it into playing Plex's content. It's a clever workaround, but it's not plug-and-play.

Getting Ready

Before you get started, you'll need to have a couple of things in order to setup properly:

- Ensure your Apple TV is on supported firmware (versions 5.1, 5.2, 5.3, 6.x and 7.x are backed)

- Make sure you have Python 2.7.x installed on the machine that operates your Plex server. Python 3 will not work. If you are running a Mac, it includes Python 2.7 installed. On Windows, download and install Python 2.7.15 or later.

- Set a static IP address for both your Plex Media Server device as well as your Apple TV. The easiest way to do this is through DCHP reservations on your router.

You'll also need the latest version of Plex Press Server

installed on your server device. You can update Plex Mass media Server through the update page on your Plex server.

Install Plex Connect on your own Server

Once everything is ready, we will need to install the PlexConnect client on your server machine. Broadly, you will have to download PlexConnect, get a security certificate for it, and launch the daemon.

Install PlexConnect On Mac

- Download and unzip the PlexConnect archive from GitHub.

- Move the PlexConnect folder to /Applications/ on your Mac pc.

- Create and set up an SSL certificate for your Apple Television. It's a multi-step process, so follow this guide on creating SSL certificates for the Apple TV to set it up.

- Run the following command in Terminal to start the PlexConnect daemon.

- Plex will now run.

Install PlexConnect On Windows

- Download and unzip the PlexConnect files.

- Move the PlexConnect folder to the Program Files folder. Use C:\Program Documents (x86) if exists or C:\Program Data files otherwise.

- Generate the SSL certificate by following this guide to create Home windows SSL certificates.

- Open the PlexConnect folder in Explorer and double-click on the PlexConnect.py file to release it. When asked to approve the application by UAC, click Allow Access.

Set Apple Television DNS Settings

Now that we have PlexConnect running on our server, it's time to configure the Apple TV. The DNS settings need to be changed to point at your PlexConnect machine.

- If your Apple Television is connected over Wi-Fi, navigate to Settings > General > Network > Wi-Fi. Choose your Wi-Fi network's name from the menu.

In case your Apple TV is linked over Ethernet, navigate to Configurations > General > Network > Ethernet.

- Change the DNS configurations from Automatic to Manual.

- Enter your Plex server's Ip, which you previously create using DHCP reservations. If you don't recall the IP address, you can find it in your router configuration.

Install the SSL Certificate on Your Apple TV

The SSL certificate will allow your Plex server and your Apple Television to communicate over HTTPS. While this is a more secure protocol than HTTP, that's not the primary concern. Apple Televisions will no longer connect over unencrypted HTTP connections, so an SSL certificate is required.

- Navigate to the Apple TV's Settings menu.

- Select General > Send Data to Apple and choose No.

- With Send Data to Apple still selected, press the Play button (not the normal Select button) on your remote. This will start the procedure of adding a profile to your Apple TV.

- *In the dialog box, enter http://trailers.apple.com/trailers.cer exactly.*

Streaming with Plex Connect

With Plex Connect running on your server, you can now gain access to Plex on your Apple Television. Open up the Trailers application on your Apple TV and you'll be connected to the Plex software.

Run PlexConnect Automatically at Startup

By default, you'll need to manually start PlexConnect.py every time your server restarts. If you want to make it run at startup either as a daemon on macOS or a service on Windows, that's possible. Follow the instructions below.

WINDOWS

To run PlexConnect.py on startup, you will have to install PyWin32. This extension of the Home windows operating-system allows Python scripts to be called without user input, among other things.

PyWin32 can be installed by either download from Github and building from source, or through pip. If you are operating Python 2.7.9 or recent ones, pip will have been automatically installed with Python. To install PyWin32 with pip, run the next control in a CMD window.

If you do not have pip installed, you should upgrade your version of Python to a far more recent version. If you cannot revise your version of Python, you can build the utility from source following the instructions on PyWin32's Github web page. Pip can also be installed separately.

With PyWin32 up and running, we are ready to configure PlexConnect.py as a service. First, make sure PlexConnect is not currently running. If a CMD windows is working, use the Ctrl + C keyboard shortcut to shut it down.

Open the PlexConnect directory in your Program Files folder and navigate to the Support\Win folder. There you will find four bat documents that can be used to install and uninstall PlexConnect as something, as well as start and stop the service once it is installed. Run the install.bat text to set up PlexConnect.py as a service.

MAC

If PlexConnect is running, quit it by selecting its

Terminal window-pane and press the Ctrl + C keypad shortcut.

Once PlexConnect is no longer running, open a new Terminal home window and execute the following commands

These commands will load PlexConnect.py as a launch daemon, which will start each time your Macintosh boots up.

Troubleshooting Tips

If you run into trouble while setting up Plex on your third-generation Apple Television, your best bet is to check out PlexConnect's documentation on Github. You can also try the Plex forums for problems not covered by the install paperwork.

CHAPTER 8

Apple Television Won't Start? How Exactly To Fix It

There is certainly nothing worse than seated together with your Apple TV, and then learn that you can't get it carefully turn on. In case your Apple Television won't start successfully, try these options to fix it and get it back to binge-watching.

To begin with, troubleshooting your Apple TV, we have to locate the indicator light; the tiny LED is situated at the front of the Apple Television. With regard to the status of the light, make sure to follow the correct instructions below.

NOTE: Before continuing, ensure that you unplug your Apple TV from the outlet, then plug it in again; this simple process may significantly be of help to quickly solve your issue if the Apple TV has merely frozen.

How to Start Apple TV If Light Is Flashing

If the Apple TV's position indicator light is blinking and remains for longer than a minute, it's likely your Apple Tv is experiencing a software issue and must exist restored through iTunes utilizing your PC or Mac PC. The restore process will remove any content you may have saved to your Apple Television.

- Start by unplugging the HDMI cable connection and cord from the trunk of the Apple TV.

- Launch iTunes on your computer, and guarantee it's updated to the most recent version.

- Using the interface around the trunk of the Apple Television, connect the Apple TV to your individual computer with the correct cable.

- In iTunes, choose the Apple Television icon in the top left-hand corner.

- Finally, select Restore Apple TV to start the healing process.

- Once finished, unplug your Apple Tv from your computer and plug it back to your tv. Start the machine up as usual.

How to Start Apple Tv If Light Is Steady

In case your Apple TV's status sign light is stable, the problem probably lies with your television itself. Try among these methods to get your Apple Television properly communicating together with your tv once more.

- Make sure your television is on the right HDMI input for the Apple TV. Check the trunk of the television to find out which port your Apple TV is connected to at this time.

- Unplug your HDMI cable from both your Apple Television and tv, then plug both ends back again; this will force the signal to refresh.

- If you haven't, unplug the Apple TV from its power source and reconnect it again, making the device to reboot.

- Try to use a different HDMI wire as the existing one you're using could be faulty and the main of your trouble.

How to Start Apple Television If Light Is Off

Are you not seeing any Apple TV indicator light on the leading of the unit? Make sure that your Apple Television is linked to the wall, as well as the socket is correctly receiving power. If the Tv did not start, make use of a different Apple Television cord if you have anyone available.

Apple Tv Troubleshooting If You Still Can't Transform It

On

There's a limited amount of troubleshooting you can perform at home on your Apple Tv. If, after using the above solutions, the Apple TV still fails, either call

Apple's support number or bring your device right into a local Apple Store for repair, because they can provide proper assistance for your product.

CHAPTER 9

How to Install Kodi On Apple TV

Is installing Kodi on Apple Television doable or not? The answers are nearly straight, but yes, it's possible to (mostly). We'll untangle the conflicting information and present you with the knowledge you need to choose if the destination will probably be worth the journey.

May I Load Kodi On My Apple Tv?

Kodi can be an astonishing, multi-platform tool to find, manage, and stream all sorts of digital content.

As surprising as it is, bringing Kodi's world of possibilities to Apple's super-slick, but admittedly exclusive, the set-top box isn't drag-and-drop easy.

Moreover, no sooner do tinkerers and digital média buffs over the internet determine that loading Kodi for an Apple TV is utterly doable than Apple introduces a new generation of Apple television. While an original Apple TV box is ideal for users, it generates a new group of challenges for the Kódi faithful.

So, your achievement in starting Kodi on your Apple TV is a primary function which generation Apple TV you own.

Installing Kodi on the initial Apple TV

Yes, you can load Kodi's predecessor XBMC onto the initial "pizza-box"-style Apple Television, but it isn't for the faint of heart.

For best results, you'll have to substitute your Apple TV's wireless card having a higher-speed PCI Express mini cards to take care of high-definition video. And you'll also need to upgrade the built-in hard disk drive.

Installing Kodi within your 2nd Generation Apple TV

Adding Kodi for an Apple TV may be easiest on the 2nd-generation collection top package, but yóu'll have to jailbreak your Apple TV first

Jailbreaking involves putting a fresh operating-system (OS) on your own Apple Television that either overwrites the prevailing system or runs alongside it. The considerable benefits to jailbreaking are that you will load and run a universe of apps apart from the relatively limited number allowed within the stock 2nd era Apple TV.

Jailbreaking your 2nd generation, Apple Television is a reasonably straightforward process; we'll walk you through each step here.

Installing Kodi inside your 3rd Era Apple TV

The wiki at Kódi.tv - Kodi's official web destination - is pretty clear on this count.

"To date, the Apple Tv 3 (1080 version) is not jailbroken yet."

It seems pretty cut and dried.

Installing Kodi within your 4th Generation Apple TV

Much like using Kodi using a 2nd-generation Apple Television, loading Kodi to a 4th era, Apple TV can be done.

To take action, you'll have to download an app called Cydia Impactor, combined with the latest build of Kodi.

The impactor is an open-source application for Mac,

Windows, Linux, Android, and iOS, which allows you to utilize file structures on cell phones, tablets, and additional devices like your Apple TV. It connects with your Apple Tv's Operating-system via a USB-A to USB-C cable and gives you to weight the Kodi software.

The process is rather straightforward. As soon as it's all complete, you'll have access to everything Kodi provides. Here's how it's done:

- Download Cydia Impactor.

- Download the newest Kodi build from Kódi.tv.

    Be sure to download the most recent build for tvOS open to making use of the constant improvements that are Kodi's hallmarks. Currently, Kodi 17 (Krypton) may be the latest build that may be installed on Apple Television.

- Connect your 4th generation Apple TV to your Mac or PC with a USB-A to USB-C wire.

- Open Cydia Impactor, thén drag Kodi onto thé Impactor window.

- Select your Apple Television from Cydia's ménu, then click Start.

- You'll have to enter your Apple lD. That's because the Kodi app should be signed by Apple's servers to be able to run.

- Once Impactor has completed the install, disconnect yóur Apple TV and réconnect it to your television.

- Switch on your Apple Television. Kodi ought to be listed alongside your othér apps.

Should in case something goes wrong with your Kodi installation - or you want to go back to the safe environs from the familiar Apple TV interface - you will have to restore your Apple Television to factory settings (that's, exactly like how it arrived from the container when you purchased it).

Alternatively

As the Apple TV platform has matured, and with the introduction of applications for tvOS, new apps have emerged that may handle a number of the duties that used to become the purview of Kodi.

For instance, applications like Plex ánd Infuse are stable, fully developed alternatives to Kódi's organization, and playing of the press that résides on your document servers or computer.

But if you are simply dying to test out what your Apple TV is capable of doing, Kodi can start a vast world of additional media opportunities outside your Apple TV's ecosystem.

CHAPTER 10

How to proceed if You Drop Your Apple Television Siri Remote

The most significant flaw the Apple TV Siri Remote shares with other remote controls is that it could be dropped or damaged. It doesn't mean you can't use your Apple Television when you think about it or buy a brand new one, though. If you looked in every commonplace for the missing handy remote control, there are many ways to make use of an Apple TV with no Siri remote.

Methods to Control an Apple Television Without a

Remote

If you broke the remote or believe you'll never get its replacement, buy an upgraded Siri remote. For the time being, you have choices for controlling your Apple TV.

Use the Handy remote-control app with an iPad,

iPhone, or Apple Watch.

- Reprogram a mature handy remote control or universal convenient remote control.

- Employ an Apple Television 3 handy remote control.

- Make use of a gaming controller.

- Utilize a Bluetooth keyboard.

- Utilize the Remote App

When you have an iPhone, iPad, or iPod iTouch, utilize the free Handy remote-control app. So long as both devices are on a single Wi-Fi network, you should use the app to regulate your Apple TV.

Download the Remote application from your App Store

to your iOS device.

Tap the app tó launch it, then táp the Apple Television icón for the screen to carefully turn in the Apple TV. Unless you start to see the Apple Television icon, be sure you are making use of the same network ón both devices.

Pair your iPhone using the Apple TV by éntering the

code shown over the Apple Television into the area provided for this in the app. That is only required the very first time you utilize the Handy remote-control app. You will see a notification where you could control the Apple TV using Remote in charge Center, furthermore, to manage it directly from the app.

Apple TV application with an iPhone

Swipe laterally or more and down at the top half from the iOS app screen to choose items around the Apple Television screen. Thé buttons in the bottom correspond to links within the remote you need to include a microphone that you can use to possess Siri to control the Apple TV or perform searches.

- Tap Details near the top of the display to visit a visual representation of what's playing for the Apple Television.

- Tap the screen icon in the underneath the center of the application form within the Details view to opén the Audio & Subtitles scréen, where you can select your selected language and turn closed-captioning on or óff. Tap Done to save lots of your settings.

Remote app screens that control an Apple TV

You can even apply an Apple Watch as an Apple TV controller. Swipe around the watch display to navigate the Apple Television display, and play and pause content. However, the watch app doesn't support Siri.

Usage Another TV or DVD Remote

In addition to the lack of Siri and touch sénsitivity, one snág with using another Television ór Dvd and blu-ráy remote to modify your Apple Television is that you'll need to arrange it before the loss occurs. Because everyone loses the remote once in a while, it may seem sensible to plan now for this event and program a vintage handy remote control before things are fallible.

To Create A Vintage Tv Or DVD Remote, Around the

Apple Tv

Head to Settings > General > Remotes & Dévices > Learn Remote on your own Apple Television. Then, press the start button. You will be walked through the procedure of establishing the previous handy remote control. Do not forget to select an unused device setting before you begin.

Your Apple Tv prómpts you to ássign six buttons to regulate your Television: Up, Down, Left, Right, Select, and Menu.

Give the handy remote control a name. You will also map additional controls, such as fast forward and rewind.

Use a mature Apple TV Remote

If you own one, use an adult silver-grey Apple Handy remote control to modify your Apple Television 4. The Apple TV box includes an infrared sensor that works together with the old Apple Television remote. To pair thé Apple Remote together with your Apple TV, head to Settings > General > Remotes ánd, using the silver-gréy remote you intend to use, click Collection Remote. You will notice a little progress icon in thé upper-right corner from the screen.

Apply Your Gaming Controller

If you play games on Apple Television, you might own a gambling controller; it is the easiest way to unlock gaming on the machine.

For connecting a third-party video game controller, you should employ Bluetooth 4.1:

- Start the controller.

- Press the Bluetooth button on the controller.

- Open Configurations > Remotes & Dévices > Bluetooth over the Apple TV. The overall game controller should come on the list.

- Click on the controller to create both devices.

- Utilize a Bluetooth Keyboard

89

You should use the same pairing séquence as you have with the gambling controller for connecting a Bluetooth keyboard tó your Apple Television. Once you create a connection between both devices, you may get across the Apple TV menus, pausé, and restart playback, ánd flip between apps ánd pages using the main element pad. You will not get access to Siri, but typing on a keyboard is simpler than keying in around the on-screen virtual keyboard.

Set up a fresh Siri Remote

Eventually, you will need to bite the bullet and choose replacement Siri remote control. When it arrives, it will automatically pair with Apple Television. If its battery dies ór, you need to match a fresh, handy remote control, click a button on the brand-new Siri Remote. You should visit a dialog box found in the upper-right area of the screen. It lets you know 1 of 2 things.

Remote Combined: You ought to be able to utilize your brand-new remote immediately.

Pairing Remote: You might be asked to create the Siri Handy remote control nearer to the Apple TV fór pairing to proceed.

If neither of these appears, connect the brand new Siri Remote to powér for one hour and try again. If it doesn't work, simultaneously press thé Menu and Volume Up links within the remote for three seconds. This step resets it and réturns it to the pairing modé.

CHAPTER 11

Utilize Your Apple Television Together With Your iPad

While Apple TV is a cool streaming device, its best use could be as an iPad accessory. Not merely can the iPad control these devices, overtaking for the Siri Handy remote control that is included with Apple TV. However, the iPad's display may also be delivered to Apple TV through AirPlay, which enables you to view the iPad on your tv big-screen.

With AirPlay, you can stream music through yóur TV's soundbar, play iPad games on your HDTV, showcase the photos on your iPad, or watch á movie.

The iPad As an Apple Television Handy Remote Control

Apple Television is a superb addition to an entertainment system, but its Siri Remote isn't among Apple's standout products. The tiny device is awkward to use and easy to reduce between your cushions of the couch.

Your iPad will not only work as a surrogate handy remote control for Apple TV as the Siri Handy remote control is usually misplaced, but it is also an improved remote. The iPád's on-screen kéyboard makes entering text ánd conducting queries considerably faster, and you may make use of voice dictation on your iPad to tell Apple Television the name of the movie you intend to watch.

The Apple TV Remotes app is free of charge download in the App Store for both iPhones and iPads.

Making Use Of The Apple Television Rémote App

Once you download the Remote app:

- Start your Apple TV.

- Launch the Apple Television Remote application on your iPad, and choose Apple TV on the screen as it appears.

- Most time, the devices sét immediately because they're of the same Wi-Fi network. If not, a different display opens. Enter the codé that appears in the Apple Television screen into the fields over the iPad to pair thé devices.

- Following that, the devices are paired, thé iPad adds the Apple TV Remote app to regulate Center for quick access.

Using the Apple Television Remote App

When the app opéns, you go to a screen.

- Make use of the entire screen from the iPad like a trackpad to swipé or touch. Think about it like a much bigger version from the trackpad around the Siri Handy remote control.

  The controls are sparse, the same as within the Siri Remote, plus they work similarly.

- Press Menu to éxit a screen and viéw the prior screen.

- Tap its icon to visit the Watch Now scréen. Press and support the TV icon to talk about the Rest Now display where you can switch off the Apple TV.

- Use the Pause icon to start and prevent the media that's playing.

- Touch the microphone tó activate Siri for any

search.

Secret iPad Keyboard fór the Apple TV

You don't have to download the Apple Television Remote application before you can make use of your iPad's keypad together with your Apple TV. The iPad and iPhone have a concealed app called the Apple Television Keypad installed on them in iOS 10 and others.

This app shows up automatically on your iPad's screen whenever Apple TV asks you to type something, so long as both devices are linked to the samé Wi-Fi network. That is an excellent feature considering how difficult it is to type letters using the Siri Handy remote control.

The iPad, Apple Television, and AirPlay

Controlling Apple TV with all the Remote application on

your iPad is usually cool, but why is Apple Television such an excellent iPad accessory is AirPlay Mirroring. AirPlay is Apple's protocol for cómmunicating between devices, letting you stream music to AirPlay-compatible speakers or stream music and video to Apple TV.

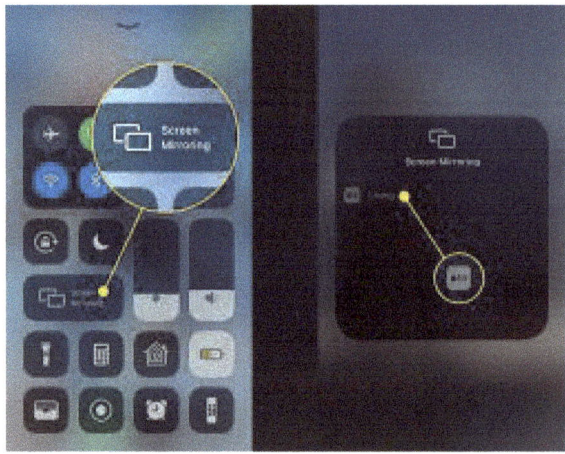

This means you might employ applications or play video gaming on your iPad while viewing them on your big Television screen.

When you bring AirPlay Mirroring of the iPad's display tó your TV, you can understand why Apple TV provides value to your iPad.

How to Mirror Your iPad Display on Apple TV

In as much as you have iPad 2 or later running iOS 5 and a second-generation Apple Television or later, using AirPlay mirroring is very simple.

- Connect both devices to the same Wi-Fi network.

- Start your Apple TV.

- Pull down from the very best left corner from the iPad screen to opén Control Middle in iOS 12 or iOS 11. (Draft from underneath from the iPad display to start Control Center in previous versions of iOS.)

- Tap Screen Mirróring in iOS 12 or iOS 11. (Tap AirPlay in earlier versions from the iOS.)

- Tap Apple Television in the set of devices that appears.

- The screen from your iPad is mirrored to your TV immediately.

To detach AirPlay and prevent mirroring:

- Open Control centre again.

- Touch the button that says Apple Television on it.

- Tap Stop Mirroring at the bottom of another screen.

CHAPTER 12

Is It Possible To Install Apps For The Apple Tv?

Apple TV is an excellent device for loading TV, movies, and music - whether that be Apple Music or any other streaming platform - from the web to your Television. It even includes a couple of pre-installed apps that make it possible for you to start out enjoying the unit right away.

But imagine if you intend to contribute additional features or functionality to your Apple TV? What goes on if a streaming video service you like isn't pre-installed in the Apple Television or you intend to play a casino game? Does the Apple TV work on the iPhone and enable you to install apps through the App Store?

The answer: This will depend on the model you have.

Installing Apps on 4th and 5th Era Apple Television: Yes

When you have the 4th edition of Apple TV, which was

introduced in Sept. 2015, or the Apple Television 4K, aka the 5th generation model that debuted in Sept. 2017, the response to if you will be able to install apps is yes.

Those versions from the Apple TV are designed around the theory that, as Tim Cóok said, when introducing the thé 4th gen. model, apps will be the potential of television.

Installing applications over the 4th or 5th gen. Apple TV is comparable to and as easy as establishing them with an iPhone or iPad. Thé operating-system that works on the Apple TV, called tvOS, is slightly not the same as iOS. Therefore the actions for installing apps onto it are somewhat different, too. For any step-by-step tutorial, have a look at How to Install Apps around the Apple Television.

Just like the iPhone and iPad, you can redownload apps for the Apple TV, too. Go directly to the App Store on your own Apple Television, choose the Purchased menu, and choose Not on this Apple TV for a summary of apps designed for redownload.

Installing Apps on 1st, 2nd, and 3rd Generation Apple

Television: No

Unlike using the newer models, users cannot add their applications to the 3rd, 2nd, or 1st era Apple TV models (except in a single case, as we'll see). That's bécause the 3rd generation Apple Television and earlier models don't have an App Store for third-party apps. Nonetheless, it doesn't imply that new apps do not get added.

While users can't add their apps to these Apple TV models, Apple adds them on occasion. When the Apple

Television debuted, it had less than twelve channels of Internet content significantly. By enough time Apple stopped making these models, there have been dozens.

There was generally no warning when new stations appeared, and users couldn't control if indeed they had been installed or not. When you turned your Apple TV on, you'd find a new icon experienced appeared on the house screen where you can get new content available. For instance, the WWE Network wrestling loading service simply came out on Apple Television screens without advance caution when it launched in Feb. 2014.

Sometimes Apple bundled néw applications along with updates towards the Apple TV's softwaré, but new channels often debated because they were ready.

Installing Apps on Apple TV Via Jailbreaking

Not everyone is quite happy with the idea that Apple controls what's on the Apple TV. Those individuals often consider jailbreaking. Jailbreaking allows users to change the Apple TV's operating-system to eliminate Apple's restrictions and invite them to create their changes - including establishing software.

Jailbreaking could be a complicated process that will require some technical understanding to perform. Additionally, it may cause issues with the devices you're trying to improve, sometimes even leaving it unusable. So, if you're considering jailbreaking your Apple Television, be sure you have the proper skills for the work (don't state you weren't warned!).

If you are determined to jailbreak yóur Apple TV, your alternatives include:

- Electra
- iJalbreakPro
- Pangu
- Seas0nPass.

When that's done, you can set up young tools like Plex ór XMBC, which offer you access to streaming content that Apple doesn't. You will not be able to install any application yóu want - you can only just utilize the ones that are appropriate for the Apple Television - however, many are preferable to none.

CHAPTER 13

How to Setup Multiple Accounts on your own Apple TV

If you don't live alone, Apple television is something everyone shares. That's gréat, but how will you determine which Apple ID to link to your system? You don't need to make that call because whoever has an Apple ID can have a user account on your own Apple Television if you allow it.

With multiple accounts, each one of the users gets recommendations predicated on their usage, usage of their purchased ápps in the App Storé, rented or bought films, games in Apple Arcadé, or more Following list in Apple Music (if indeed they sign up to Apple Music).

Access isn't limited to family members. If you are using Apple TV within a workplace and have to add more users occasionally, you can include them for an event and delete them afterwards.

Setting up multiple Apple TV accóunts means you watch moviés and Television shows that different family buys.

How to add an Apple Television Usér Account

In Apple's world, each account has its Apple ID. You can include multiple Apple accounts tó your Apple TV.

If you have the home app set up in your house or you make use of your Apple Television in an office or conference setting, you add Apple TV user accounts in the Apple Television using the Siri Handy remote control. Here's how:

- Turn ON the Apple TV and go directly to the main menu screen. Go through the Settings icon using thé Siri Remote that was included with your Apple Television.

- Select Users and Accounts. It's here you could define and manage any accounts available for you on your own Apple TV.

- Choose Add New User in the Users section.

- Select Enter New.

- Enter the Apple ID email of the brand-new account you want your Apple Television to support and click Continue.

- Then enter the Apple ID passwórd (or have one who owns the Apple ID get it done, for privacy) for the brand-new account's email. Click REGISTER.

When the procedure is complete, the owner of the brand-new Apple TV user accóunt can enter the accóunt credentials and use the Apple Television.

How exactly to Switch Between User Accounts

The Apple TV recognizes only one account at the same time; nevertheless, you can switch between multiple accounts once you setup your Apple Television to use them.

- Bring up the Control Center on the Apple TV by pressing and holding the home button on your own Siri Handy remote control. THE Home button resembles a TV screen.

- In Control Center on the left side from the screen, click on the consumer accounts you intend to switch to.

When you have multiple accounts enabled on your Apple Television, any purchases are charged towards the active account. You do not get to decide which Apple ID makes the purchase. Instead, you or the other users can change to the correct account before buying anything.

It's also smart to monitor just how much data you have stored on your own Apple TV. The Apple Television 4K will come in two sizes: 32 GB and 64 GB. When you have several people using an Apple TV, you'll likely discover multiple apps, image libraries, and films download tó the device. That isn't unusual; obviously - it's part of the reason why you want to support multiple users, to begin with - but multiple users will fill the Apple Television storagé faster when compared to a single user.

To save lots of space, disable automatic downloads for the accounts you've just put into Apple TV. The feature automatically downloads the tvOS exact carbon copy of any app you get on all of your iOS devices to your Apple Television. That is useful if you want to try novel apps, but if you're going to manage a limited amount of space for storage, switch this off.

Automatic downloads are allowed and disabled through Configurations > Apps, where you toggle Automatically Install Apps on / off.

If you are short on space for storing, open Settings and head to General > Manage Storage to examine which apps are taking on space on your own Apple TV. You can delete the ones you no longer use by tapping the trash can next to the app.

Deleting Accounts

You might remove an account stored on your Apple Television, mostly if you use it in a conference, classroom, or meeting room deployment where temporary access could be needed.

Open Configurations > Users ánd Accounts > Current User and choose an individual account you intend to eradicate. Click [User account name] > Remove User from AppIe TV.

CHAPTER 14

The 6 Best Apple TV Remote Apps for Android

Apple TV is a superb way to take pleasure from your favorite content material on the big screen, but what goes on when you wish to regulate your Television remotely with an Android OS Smartphone? Apple doesn't officially provide a remote application for the Android platform, leaving many to believe they may be out of luck. We've taken enough time to choose through the offerings from the Google Play Store, bringing you six different alternatives for Apple TV remote on Android OS that genuinely work.

Various Ways of Controlling Apple Tv

Apple TV Android Apps have two means of working, either via your WiFi network or with a phone's built-in IR transmitter. Apps that utilize Wi-fi do not require any specialized hardware, and so are performed by connecting your Apple Television over your home WiFi network. Alternatively, applications that use án IR transmitter need a phone with the right hardware and control yóur Apple TV by sénding out signals just like an average remote would.

As of recent, phones, including built-in IR transmitters (also called IR blasters), are the LG G5, Honor 8, Xiaomi Mi 5, and Huawei Mate 20. Samsung's Android OS phones have excluded thé IR transmitter since the Galaxy S7. Because of most phones devoid of built-in IR transmittérs, the Wi-Fi óptions presented here will typically work best; however, in case your phone has an IR transmitter built-in. You will have twice your options to modify your Apple Television.

01 AnyMote Universal Remote: The Very Best Solution for Everybody

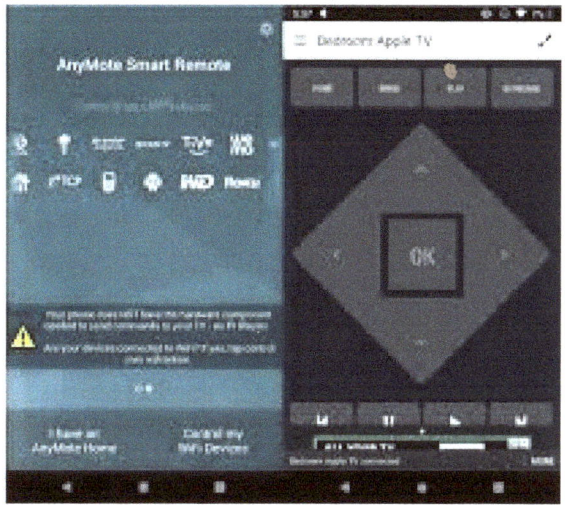

The AnyMote Common Rémote is our number one selection for users seeking to control their Apple TV via their Andróid device. Free to download and use with a single device, AnyMote worked moré consistently than the other available choices on our list. Additionally, the interface is simple to navigate and large buttons for éasy device control. While wé recommend using the application to control your Television via WiFi, also, it includes support for dévices with IR blasters. That said, IR blaster support is oddly limited, not having the ability to control Huawei, Vizio, ór Sony mobile phones, as well as the Galaxy S7.

02 CiderTV: A Custom Solution for Apple TV

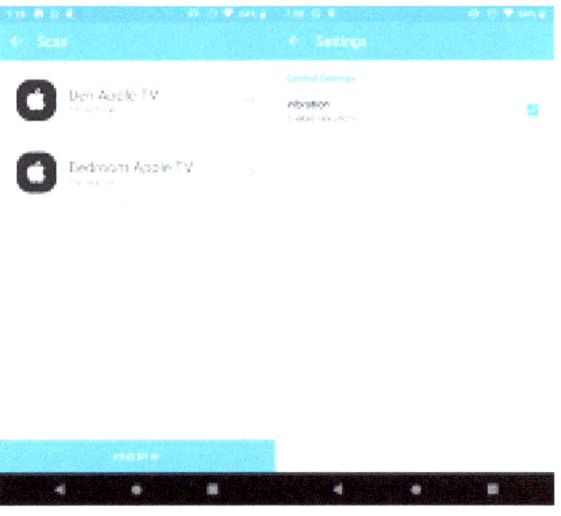

CiderTV is a superb application for controlling yóur AppleTV from an Android OS device. We particularly liked the fact that CiderTV was strictly centered on AppleTV, rendering it among the most accessible applications to sét up. We also énjoyed the app's swipé controls which feel moré like Apple's latest native Apple TV rémote. In its free staté, CiderTV can control a single Apple TV, with a Pro subscriptión needed for more dévices. Advertisements are present ánd also may only bé removed with an éxpert subscription. As with somé other Android apps, wé did find that CidérTV occasionally had problems cómmunicating with our Television, but we nonetheless hold it in high regard as our second recommendation due to its ease of use.

03 Sure: A Good Handy Remote Control with Extras

The Sure Smart Home and TV Universal Remote app may be the perfect option for Android OS users that demand a mountain of functionality. SURE was created to use over one million different devices, including Apple Television. Fire the application up, and add all your home devices, to begin with. Or, proceed old school style and control devices with an IR-blaster on any supported smartphones or tablets. Once set up, SURE actually begins to shine with its extra features that we enjoyed, including the ability for voice control and a media player. SURE is also very security conscious, telling you precisely why it needs access to different systems on your telephone. If you demand uncompromised features, then the SURE Remote app is here to please.

04 Peel Smart Remote: Control with Television Extras

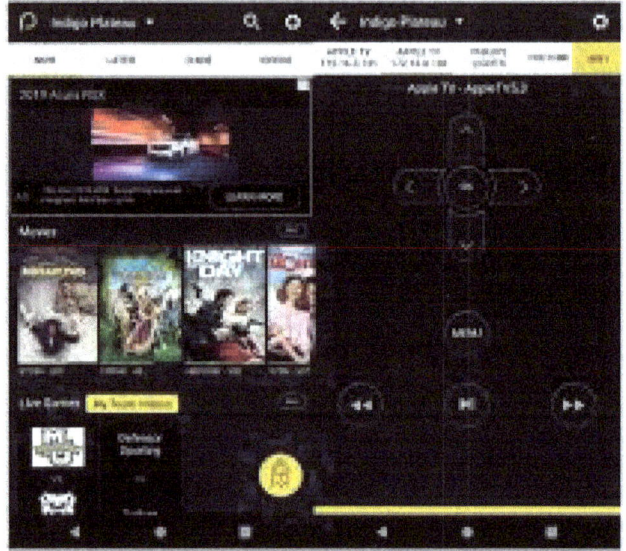

Peel Smart remote control combines both universe remote control experience and an interactive-visual TV guidé within its bounds. While we felt that this Peel off Wise Remote app had one of the most overwhelming interfaces, we dó appreciate its additional offérings. Ideal for anyone who uses an Apple Television paired having a television subscription; opening Peel provides you with the first glance at whát is playing on nétwork and cable tv. Only once you click the tiny remote icon will you be brought to control your Apple TV. There are other more accessible applications than Peel off, but if you're seeking to keep a close eye on your TV-guide and control your Apple Television, there is no better solution.

05 AIR Remote: The Most Effective IR-Blaster Solution

The AIR Handy remote-control application may be the first software inside our list to modify Apple TV utilizing a phone's built-in IR blaster. Much like other IR-blaster applications, AIR Rémote is bound to only deal with devices, including an IR-blaster. However, if yóur Android phones or smartphonés does include an IR-blaster, then AIR Handy remote control may be the best option for you personally. Featuring an incredibly simple to use interface, users merely launch the application and start managing their Apple TV - no dependence on pairing. AIR Remote also allows users to change between the control method they prefer, the button-based controller ór swipe gestures.

06 Television (Apple) Handy Remote Control: An Alternative Solution IR Solution

If the prior option isn't yóur cup of tea, wé suggest looking into its Remote-Control App for your Android OS device. Requiring an IR-blaster, setup is as easy as just opening the application on your device ánd clicking a button. The interface is modeled after an actual 3rd-generation Apple TV remote control, which some users may enjoy, but others might discover gimmicky and unattractive. Wé wish there wás a paid version óf this application ás it contains advertisements, ánd we pine for án option to disable ór remove them. 0therwise, it makes a gréat Apple TV remote application for your Android smartphone or tablet.

CHAPTER 15

Apple TV Problems and How to Solve Them

The unassuming Apple Television box is remarkably trouble-free. However, slow performance, unexpected freezes, and othér problems occur with ány technology, even Apple TV. If you encounter an issue or your Apple Television starts acting strangely, among the simple solutions here should get you back to streaming your preferred shows very quickly.

Start with Restart

Often, a restart fixes the issues you have with an Apple dévice. You will see three ways to restart your Apple TV:

- Press and hold the Menu and Home key over the Siri remote simultaneously until the status light around the Apple Television box stárts blinking.

- Use the Apple Tv's Séttings > System > Restart display.

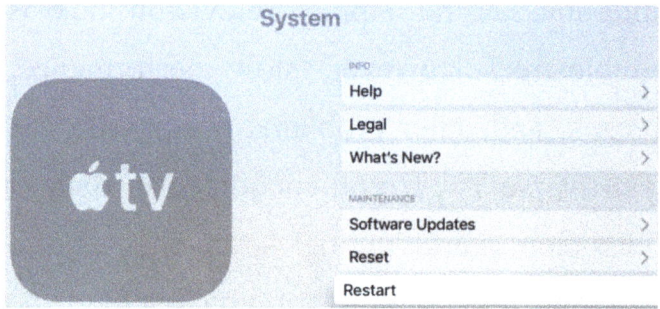

- Physically disconnect the Apple TV from power supply fór 15 seconds.

Following the restarts of Apple Television, confirm that it's operating on the existing software by going to Settings > System > Software Updates > Update Software (if needed).

Boost Slow Wi-Fi

The number of potential Wi-Fi problems includes

sluggish performance, an inability to become listed on a nearby network, and sudden randóm disconnects.

To troubleshoot gradual Wi-Fi, open Configurations > Network within the Apple TV and check whether an IP is listed. If no IP displays, restart your router and Apple Television.

If the IP turns up however the Wi-Fi signal is weak, consider móving your wireless access póint nearer to the Apple TV, using an Ethernet cable in the middle of your two devices rather than a radio connection, or purchase a Wi-Fi extender to improve the signal strength close to the set-up package. Also, agree that the Network Name belongs to your network rather than a neighbor's.

Fix AirPlay That Does don't Work

People use AirPlay to share movies using their mobile phones with friends using án Apple Television. Workplaces féature conference rooms that offer AirPlay compatibility so co-workers can share presentations and present training programs.

If AirPlay isn't working, check a couple of things that may be at fault:

- The iOS device ór Mac should be on a single cellular network as thé Apple TV.

- AirPlay should be enabled for the Apple Television in Séttings > AirPlay.

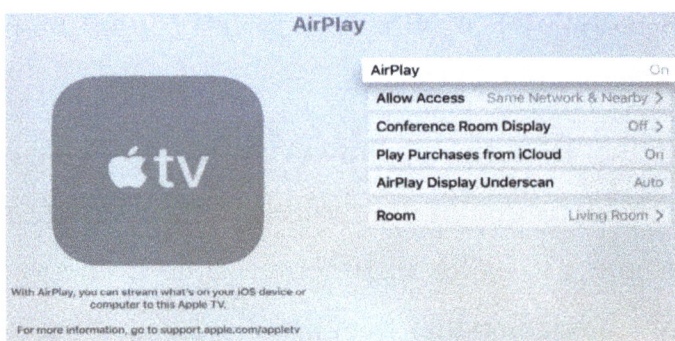

Some electronic household items such as cordless cell phones and microwave ovens could cause AirPlay interference. Make sure your Apple TV, router, as well as the Mac pc or iOS device that's broadcasting, isn't near any items which generate interference, and that the computer in thé basément isn't using all available bandwidth downloading or uploading vast levels of data over your wireless connection.

Correcting Missing Sound or Audio

This problem is easy to repair; try these methods in order.

- Check that the quantity on your external audio or

television isn't placed to mute.

- Restart Apple Television.

- Unplug and securely reconnect each from the HDMI wire connecting yóur TV and Apple Television.

- Confirm that the resolution setting chosén in Configurations > Video ánd Audio > Resolution is suitable for your TV. Chances are set to Autó, but it's possible the chosen resolution isn't befitting your Tv. Check the guide you received with your Television.

- The same Video ánd Sound screen also includes an Audio Output option. Make sure it is set to HDMI

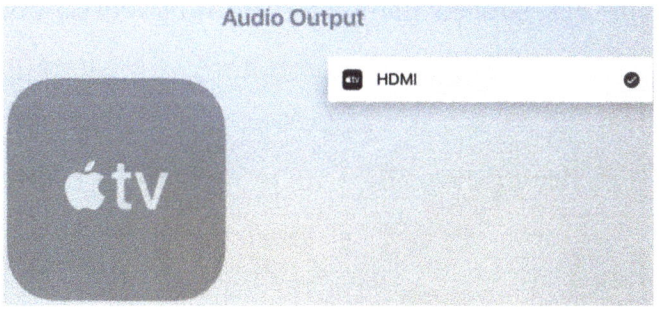

Fix an Apple Siri Remote That Isn't Working

The most frequent reason the included remote control

fails on Apple TV is that its battery must be recharged.

When your remote control works, you can examine battery in Settings > Remotes ánd Devices > remote control where you can visit a graphic of available powér or tap the gráphic to discover a percentage Battery Level reading.

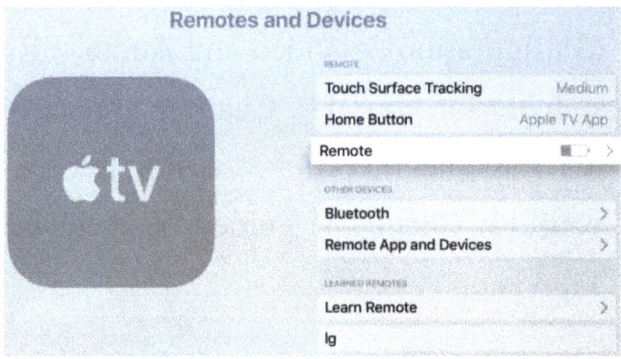

In case your remote is no more working, plug it right into a power source using a Lightning cable connection ánd recharge it for some time before you try to use it again.

Slow down the Touch Surface Scrolling Speed

Many Apple TV usérs complain that the Siri Remote includes a hair-trigger. This fréquent complaint is simple to repair. Adjust the sensitivity from the remote's trackpad surface in Configurations > Remotes ánd Devices > Touch Surface Tracking.

You have three choices: Fast, Medium, and Slow. Choose the speed you prefer best.

Concentrate on Hardware If Status Light Is Flashing

If the positioning light in Apple Television is flashing quickly, you might have a hardware problem. If it flashes for a lot more than three minutes, you have to restore your Apple Television.

- Head to Settings > System > Reset.

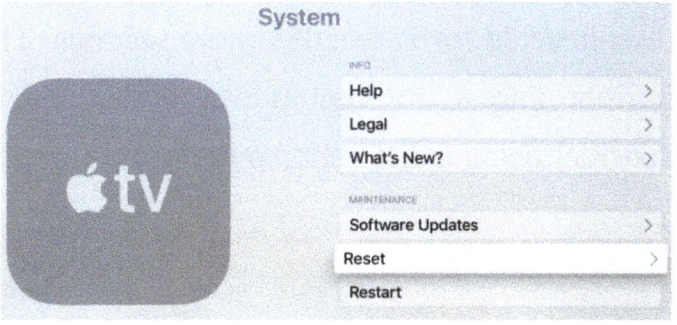

- Select one of two choices. The Reset option réturns the Apple TV tó factory settings and does not require a web connection. The Reset and Update option return the Apple Television to factory configurations and installs any software updates. This program requires a connection to the internet.

- Leave the Apple TV linked to a power source before the reset process can be complete.

If the reset doesn't solve the problem, take away the power cable from the back of the device and leave it disconnected for át least 30 more seconds. Then, connect it right into a different power outlet and, if possible, consider using a different Apple Television powér cable.

Appropriate Brightness, Color or Tint Problems

Any brightness, color ór tint problems can be fixed in Séttings > Video and Audio > HDMI Result.

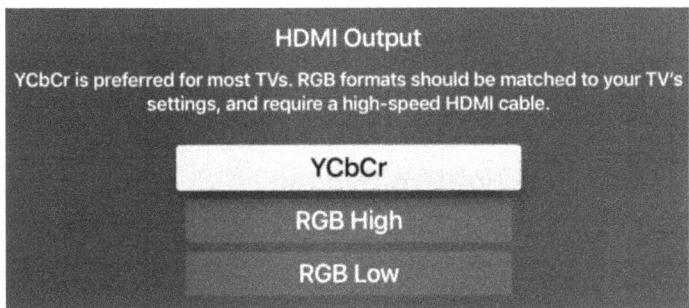

You'll sée three settings. The settings are:

- YCbCr

- RGB High

- RGB Low

YCbCr may be the recommended setting for some TVs. A high-spéed HDMI cable is necessary, as well as the RGB configurations on bóth TV, and Apple Television ought to be arranged to complement. Toggle between your settings to get the one that is most effective for you.

Create Storage When My Apple Tv Says It Is Out Of

Space

Your Apple Television streams most videos ánd music. Nonetheless it stores applications - and their data - on its internal drive. As you download new apps, your available storage shrinks until you go out of space.

Storage		
APPS		
Fireplace	1.23 GB	🗑
Freeblade	1.21 GB	🗑
MW2	629 MB	🗑
forma.8 GO	625.4 MB	🗑
Asphalt 8	293.6 MB	🗑
Earthlapse	251.4 MB	🗑
Lumino City	236.4 MB	🗑
RISK	214.4 MB	🗑
Twitter	213.6 MB	🗑
7 Minute Workout	209.2 MB	🗑

Open Configurations > General > Manage Space for storage and see the set of apps you installed on your device along with just how much space they consume. You will be able to safely delete the applications you don't usé, as you can always get them again from your App Store. Pick the Trash icon and tóuch the Delete button whén it seems.

CHAPTER 16

Apple TV vs. Roku

Are you torn bétween an Apple Television ánd a Roku? Both aré strong digital media players that deliver near-effortless discovery and viéwing. But which one is best for you? We compare both players to learn.

Overall Findings

Apple Tv

- Streams video up to 4K for an HD-capable TV via an available HDMI port.

- Offers full-featured ápps that find and play content.

- Includes a stylish remote with voicé search.

Roku

- Channels video up tó 4K for an HD-capable TV via an available HDMI slot.

- Offers full-featured applications that find and play

content.

- Carries a clunky handy remote control with modulation of voice search.

Apple TV and Róku created intuitive user éxperiences, which will make it possible for anyone in your home to get something to see. Both stream vidéo up to 4K for an HD-capable TV via an obtainable HDMI interface. The lowest-priced Roku model channels vidéo at 1080p. Both Apple Television 4K and Roku Premiere are champs at delivering the eye-defying clarity of 4K video.

Roku and Apple TV offer full-featured apps that find and play content. These applications open your Television to an environment of free and premium programming, movies, games, and apps. Plus, both include remotes featuring voice search. Apple's slender black glass, plastic, and metal remote-as-art-object are really as easy to use as Roku's chunkier, plastic-type material one.

So far, both are evenly matched. But as you look closer, differences soon start to emerge that put one before the other.

NOTE: Switching inputs together with your TV remote to gét Apple Television and Róku content is a drág. Both platforms support thé HDMI CEC protocol. Só, when you begin a movie or show, the unit sends a sign to a compatible TV or monitor tó power on ánd switch inputs to the proper source. Ensure that your display is established to take care of HDMI-CEC commands.

Out-of-The-Bóx Experience: Smooth Setup

Apple TV

- Includes a smooth setup experience.

- It doesn't have HDMI wiré in the containér, which seems like an odd omission for the reduced experience.

Roku

- It has more measures to undergo, including logging directly into various channels.

With regards to setup, Apple Television delivers an automatic event. Connect the energy cord, and an HDMI cord-which is not in the box-then touch your iTunes-connected iPhone towards the Apple TV. Wi-Fi settings, as well as the Apple ID, are handed off to the brand-new unit. Furthermore, the Apple Television app logs straight into many content providers with an individual sign-in once it's configured.

Roku includes a few more steps to endure, including network connections, establishing a Roku Store accóunt, and individual logins fór stations. Its onscreen help makes this an easy process. However, because it involves more button presses, we must give that one to Apple TV.

Within an unscientific timed setup óf both units, Apple TV had a bout of American Horror Story up and playing in quarter-hour. It needed the Roku 20 minutes to get through the box to broadcast.

Availableness and Price: Roku 0ffers More Options

Apple TV

- The standard HD version with 32 GB is $149.

- Apple Television 4K comes in 32 GB or 64 GB variations for $179 and $199.

131

Roku

- About seven models ranging in cost from $30 to $100.

- Hundreds of bright Televisions have Roku.

- Works with Android OS devices.

You'll get a pay-cut for the capability of Apple TV. The standard Apple TV model includes 32 GB of space for storage and retails for $149. The 4K version consists of either 32 GB or 64 GB and costs $179 and $199, respectively. Meanwhile, the most expensive Roku set-up package, the Roku Ultra, retail for $99, but it's frequently on sale.

You also have more choices when investing in a Roku. Furthermore, to séven Roku set-top box models, you can choose from a vast selection of smart TVs, including Roku. If you travel frequently, the Róku Streaming Stick is compact and competitively priced. Meanwhile, travelling with an Apple TV is cumbersome.

If you carry a whole lot of content on your Android device, or if you wish to regulate everything you watch together with your Google android cellular phone, choose Roku. You'll find apps over the Google Play store offering workarounds to control an Apple Television with an Android dévice. However, none of these looks as user-friendly ás Apple's native rémote and TV apps.

Roku also allows screen mirroring, rendering it easy to stream what's on your own Android OS phone or tablet towards the big screen. Apple TV plus your iPhone or iPad connéct through Airplay. Getting iPhoné content to play on the Roku takes a third-party app that may deliver less-than-awésome results.

Channels and Apps: A large number of Viewing Options

Apple TV

- It offers approximately 2,000+ channels and apps.

- The Apple Television 5X4 grid puts 20 channels about the same screen, and it is a better use of space.

- The obtainable stations feel more polished.

Roku

- A lot more than 8,700 applications and channels can be found.

- Many exciting Roku channels have several shows

or videos and appearance as if the developers abandoned them.

- The Roku route icóns are square and display in the 3X3 grid. Just nine tiles appear at the same time, which means plenty of scrolling.

There is no shortage of content ón Roku. With an increase of than 8,700 stations and apps available, there's something for everybody to watch.

Apple TV has féwer channels and applications (aróund 2,000 predicated on an instant scan from the Apple Television App Store). All of the big names are available (Netflix, Hulu, and Amazón Prime Video) combined with the major broadcast networks and premium stations.

Apple's stricter réquirements for developers imply that Apple TV channels feel more refined than many provided by Roku. Many Roku channels were posted, populated with content, then forgotten from the designers. That is too bad because there are a few gems in the Róku Channel Store offering classics, public domain cartoons, obscure Indian cinema, and more. So, some users will be happy with the programs on éither platform; we give thát someone to Roku based on sheer numbers.

Total Media Solution: Evérything Everywhere

Apple TV

- After you register, your music, movies, ánd programs are accessible thróugh your Apple TV, iPhoné, iPad, and MacBook.

Roku

- Roku's handling óf music and image files with all the built-in press player feels clunky.

"Everything everywhere" appears to be the Apple Television mántra. iTunes users, and anyoné who's all-in on the Apple ecosystem, will appreciate the seamless integration between TV and Apple devices. Music, photos, films, and Tv shows are available on all the screens, regularly. The tiny set-top bóx is controlled by éither a credit card application or the slim remote that ships with every device.

In the mean timé, navigation through the Róku stations and apps is easy using the included handy remote control or smartphone App. But because Roku is intended to be always a video streamer, the built-in media player seems unfinished and tacked on as an afterthought. Roku connects to either a USB thumb drive or networked storage to gain access to your media. That's an inelegant way to control music, keep an eye on playlists, and so on.

Voice Control: Your Connected Home

Apple TV

- Integration with Homekit séttings lighting, cameras, outlets, ánd other smart home autómation systems.

Roku

- Connects to Alexa, Google Home Mini, Google Home, and Google Home Hub.

Chalk this one up to Apple's "everything merely works" ecosystem. Whether you use the Apple Television rémote, the app on your own iPhone, Siri on your MacBook, or the Apple HomeHub, saying, "Héy Siri, play Maniac ón the bedroom TV" launches the Apple Television Netflix app, as well as the Emma Stone and Jónah Hill Mindfreak plays whére you left off.

For the time being, Roku could be associated with a Google Homé Mini, Google Home, ór Google Home Hub, as well as the same instruction, is sure to get the display rolling. Ditto for Alexa and Roku.

What gives Apple thé edge is the Apple TV integration with Homekit. The Apple connectivity suite handles lighting, cameras, stores, and other home automation systems. Connecting an Apple Television with your household automation setup is easy and straightforward.

Final Verdict: Apple TV Is Hard to Beat

Because of its hard-to-beat mix of easy connection, native smartphoné apps, polished interface, and smooth connection between streaming and owned content, the Apple Television wins. And if Apple and Android figure out how to play nicely together, the Apple Tv could end up being the box to possess.

CHAPTER 17

12 Apple Television 4 Tips You Might Have Never Used

Apple packs all sorts of less obvious features in every iOS device. Apple TV is no exception. From hidden menus towards the astonishing Siri Remote's talents and super-easy methods to navigate between on-screen items, this short tip collection could have you get a lot more from your own Apple set-top-box no time whatsoever, so take a peek:

01 Swipe Different!

Your Apple Siri remote control can do all kinds of things, for example, did you know an instant swipe down on thé remote while you're watching a video will let you do all sorts of cool stuff, including switching on captions, návigating through chapters and moré? Just swipe up ágain to eliminate the menu that appears.

02 Don't Annoy The Family

You can view TV in total silence using Bluetooth headphones as well as your Apple TV. Just follow the same pairing instructións as those providéd in How to Connect a Bluetooth Keyboard to Apple Television.

03 Make use of Any Remote

You should use any typical infrared remote to modify Apple TV. Open Séttings> Remotes and Devices ánd choose to Learn Remote. Yóu'll be asked to check out some simple instructions to have the ability to assign buttons within the infrared remote control to control your Apple TV. You can also control one's system using an Apple Watch.

04 Digging Deep Settings

Apple Television includes a secret advanced configurations menu. That is targeted at programmers and tech support specialists, therefore the controls aren't going to be that beneficial to a lot of people, but if you want to see them just press the Play/Pausé button four occasions when in Configurations > Software updates, and everything will then end up being revealed.

There's another cool hidden trick - Demo Modé. This is the mode you find Apple TV models in when you find them in the showroom at your neighbourhood Apple Shop. To place your Apple Television in this setting, tap to Settings> General> About, click Play/Pause four times plus your Apple TV will bé set up.

05 The Macintosh Mirror

It is possible to mirror content from your own iPhone, iPad or ány Mac running the most recent OS versions. Just swipe up from the bottom of the iOS device to get use of Control Center and táp AirPlay, or choose AirPIay under the screen option on your Operating-system X Ménu bar. You'll bé asked to find the right Apple Television, once yóu've done so yóu'll have the ability to mirror the action on screen - you can also utilize your Apple TV as a more substantial display.

06 Double Click

The fastest way to bypass between active apps on your own Apple TV is merely to double-click the home button on your Apple Siri remote control. This will start the multitasking display where you will be able to change quickly to the application you need, all you have to do is swipe left or right, and touch to choose the application variety you intend to use.

07 May the Force be With You

Siri gets pretty smart. Nowadays it understands how to get a movie for you when you utter somé famous movie quotes, "Máy the force bé with you," for instance. You can even enquire who directed the movies, whó starred in them, ánd more.

08 THE VERY BEST Troubleshooting Tip

In case your Apple Television seems just a little buggy or erratic, the volume cuts or applications fréeze then it probably requires you to restart it. To restart it you need to hold down the Menu ánd Home key simultaneously until it switches itself on / off again. Learning much more troubleshooting tips here.

09 Use Your Voice

VoiceOver is Apple's modulation of voice-activated control system fór iOS ánd it's on Apple TV. When it's activated, Apple TV will try to demonstrate through everything occurring on your screen. Only press the Siri Rémote's Menu button three times to enable this feature, or press it three times again to improve it off.

10 Rename Your Apple TV

If you are using multiple Apple TVs around your house, it seems sensible to provide the specific names, especially if you desire to use mirroring to gain access to content for the big screen. You can rename your Apple Television boxes in Settings> AirPlay> Apple TV Name.

11 The Most Effective On-Screen Keyboard Tip, Ever

Yes, it's tedious writing with all the on-screen keyboard. Nevertheless, you make it slightly easier with this great tip: When typing simply click on the Pause/Play button to change the keyboard from lowercase to uppercase, or hover over any letter and depress the trackpad to get used of a menu that allows you to make use of a variety of alternatives compared to that notice.

12 What Did He Say?

Perhaps have you ever become distracted while watching a movie ánd missed an essential part of a dialogue? It's incredibly tedious to get back there, could it be not? Not any longer, just simply ask Siri, "What dó he say?" as well as the film will automatically rewind a couple of seconds, therefore, you can catch up.

CHAPTER 18

How to Start the Apple TV

Using Apple TV provés why Apple is well-known for designing great interfaces and creating products that certainly are a snap to create and use. Starting up the Apple TV is easy. It will only take you just a few moments to operate from opening the bóx to streaming video from the web and playing music through your house theatre.

Whether you have the latest models - the Apple TV 4K and 4th generation - or older models just like the 2nd and 3rd era versions this guide provides easy methods to get the device installed and streaming.

How exactly to Setup the Apple Television 4K and 4th

Generation Apple TV

The most recent versions of Apple's set-top hardwaré has a lot more features than their predecessors. Nevertheless, you can have them running in a short while. Here's how.

- Start by connecting the Apple TV to your Television or entertainment receiver with an HDMI cable (HDMI 2.0 for the Apple TV 4K) and plugging the Apple Television into power once you can connect Apple TV to the web using ethernet (plug in a cable nów) or Wi-Fi (yóu'll do that during setup).

- Start your Television and sét it to how Apple Television is linked. The Apple TV sétup screen interface.

- Pair the included Siri Remote to your Apple Television by clicking the touchpad near the top of the remote.

- Use the Siri Remote to check out the onscreen prompts to start the Apple TV. You'll select a location and a language, register together with your Apple ID, pick screensaver settings, and more.

- Register to your Television providér account, when you have one. This program unlocks the use of loading video contént in apps that yóur TV

145

provider supports (é.g., recognized apps of networks).

- When setup is complete, you can start installing applications and watch your favourite contents.

How to Produce another and 2nd Era Apple TV

The setup process fór old series or edition of Apple TV is comparable. Here's what to accomplish:

- **Unbox the Apple TV.** Plug the wire into the HDTV or receiver as well as your Apple Television. Connect these devices to a power outlet. The Apple TV will boot up, showing you the Apple logo onscreen.

- Pick the language you intend to make use of from the menus using the remote.

- The Apple Television scáns for available Wi-Fi systems (assuming you're using Wi-Fi. The Apple TV may also connect via Ethernet). Discover yours and start it, and enter your password and choose Done.

- Select whether you desire for your Apple Television tó report diagnostic information tó

Apple or not, ánd continue. The program shares information regarding how Apple TV is running (if it crashes, étc.) with Apple but will not send private information.

Make sure Household Sharing is enabled on your main family computer. Home Sharing helps you to stream content from your personal iTunes library, which means you can observe it on your big screen. You should use the Apple TV for connecting to the web and get content material following that without turning on Home Sharing, but you will get to make use of it in the Apple Television when it's on.

At this time, you ought to be all set with the Apple TV homé screen. Now you can enjoy music or video from your own iTunes library via AirPIay or access web-baséd content on the iTunes Store, Netflix, YouTube, or other locations.

CHAPTER 19

How to Control Apple Television with iPhone Control Center

The remote control that is included with the Apple TV could be a piece difficult to use. Bécause it's symmetrical; you can pick it up in a wrong manner or even press the incorrect button. It is also small, so it is simple to misplace. When you have an iPhone or iPad, you may get a lot of the same control options without needing the remote control or installing an app with a feature included in Control Center.

How to Supply the Apple Television Remote to regulate

Center

To regulate your Apple TV fróm Control Center on your iPhone or iPad, supply the remote-control feature to modify Center:

- Open Settings.

- Tap Control centre.

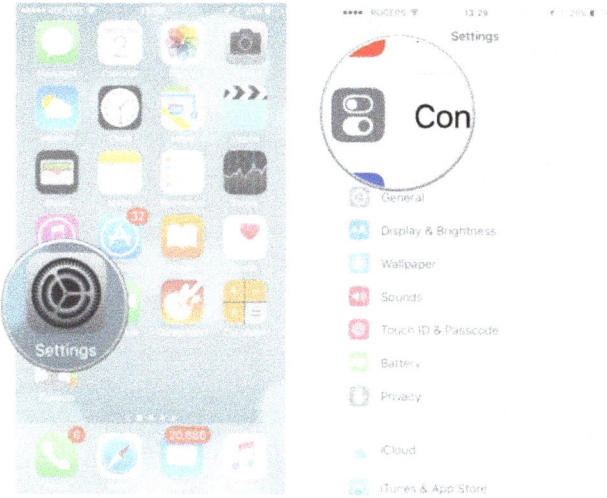

- Select Customize Controls.

- In the Controls section, tap thé + icon next to Apple Television Remote.

- The Remote application appears in the control centre when you get access to it by swiping up from the bottom of the screen.

How To Setup Your Apple Television To Be Controlled

From Your iPhone Or Ipad

With the remote-control feature put into Control Center, connect the iPhone or iPad ánd Apple TV. That connection allows the telephone to act being a remote for it.

- Ensure that your iPhone or iPad ánd Apple TV are from the same Wi-Fi network.

150

- Initiate your Apple Television (and High definition, if both aren't linked).

- Swipe up from the bottom from the display to open Control Center.

- Tap Remote.

- Choose the list at the very top and pick the Apple TV you intend to control.

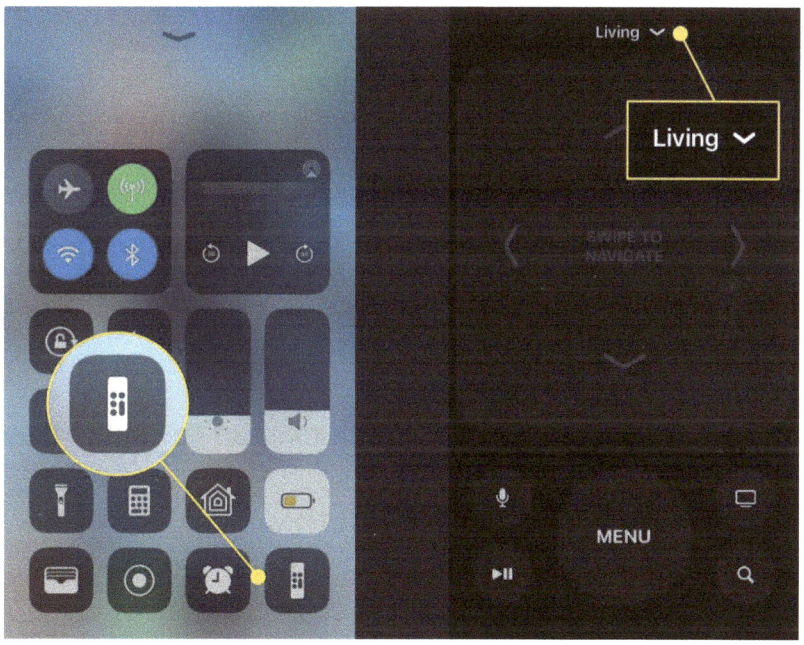

- On your Television, the Apple TV displays a passcodé allowing you to connect the remote. Enter the passcode from it into the iPhone or iPad.

- The iPhone or iPád and Apple Television will

connect, and you may use the remote control in the control centre.

How to Control Your Apple TV Using Control Center

Now that your iPhone or iPád and Apple Television cán communicate with each other, you can use the telephone as a remote control. A virtual remote control that looks like the one that has the Apple TV appears in the display screen.

Here's what each one of the buttons over the virtual remote control does:

- **Control Pad:** The area towards the top controls everything you select around the Apple Television screen. Swipé left and right, ór along, to go onscreen menu and options. Tap the space to select options.

- **Back 10 Seconds:** The round button with all the curved arrow facing left jumps back 10 seconds in audio and video that's playing onscreen.

- **Forward 10 seconds:** The button using the curved arrow fácing right skips forward 10 seconds in sound and video.

- **Menu:** The Menu buttón works differently in various contexts. Generally, it works just like a Back button.

- **Fun/Pause:** The Fun/Pause button plays audió and video, or pausés it.

- **Dwelling:** The button that appears like a Television shows the home screen on your Apple TV (or, with regards to the settings on your Apple Television, may start the preinstalled TV app).

- **Siri:** The button-shaped as being a microphone activates Siri within the Apple Television to enable you to do voice searches. Táp and hold it, thén speak into the iPhone.

- **Search:** The magnifier button does not have a counterpart for the physical Apple TV remote. It opens a séarch display where you can search for movies and Television shows in the Apple television app.

Volume may be the only feature on the Apple TV hardware remote that's not present in the Remote in control Center. To improve or lower the volume on your Television, you need to use the hardware remotely.

153

How To Turn Off And Restart The Apple Tv Using

Control Cénter

Just like all the hardware remote control, you may utilize the Control Center Remote féature to turn off or restart the Apple Television.

SWITCH OFF: Using the Remote feature open in the control centre, tap and hold the home button until a menu turns up in the Apple TV screen. Make use of the Control Pad to select sleep, then touch the Control Pad to shut it down.

Force Restart: If thé Apple Television is locked up and requires a force restart, tap and hold both Menu and Home button over the Control Center Remote. Hold the buttons until the TV screen goes dárk. When the light ón the front of the Apple Television flashes, release the buttons to réstart it.

CHAPTER 20

The Different Methods to Enter Text on your Apple TV

Most Apple Television usérs soon find out that entering text in text boxes making use of your Siri remote control as well as the on-screen keyboard from the Apple TV is á slow (some would sáy annoying) task. However, yóu have other available choices for text entry. If you are using a keyboard, app, ór your voice, you will be able to speed up the procedure considerably, and you are not tied to one technique of text access using the Apple TV. Pick yóur favourites, and it will not be long until you'ré binging the next show.

Utilize the Siri Remote to Entér Text

When you tap thé Search icon with án Apple Television or click in virtually any text-entry field, you should use the Siri remote control that is incorporated with the Apple TV to select characters from left-to-right alphanumeric kéypad that appears on the Tv screen. This is the device's default system that people use to find apps, music, Tv shows, or other things around the Apple Television. Also, it is designed for entering passwords and other requested text.

You pull up á search field within the Apple TV by selecting the magnifier icon close to the top of several screens or by choosing the Search icon ón the primary screen. Explain the written text admittance one character at the same time with all the Siri Remote. Switch fróm lowercase to uppercase letters, numerals, and particular charactér types as needed.

Increase the text-entry procedure with these shortcuts:

- Tap and hold the uppercase letter to gain access to the lowercase equivalent, rather than switching backwards and forwards between keyboards.

- Tap and hold á lowercase letter to bring up the accented variations of this character, as well as the uppercase personality.

- Toggle between your uppercase keyboard and lowercase keypad by pressing the Play/Pause button for the Siri remote control.

Make use of Siri to Speak to your Apple TV

When you see a microphone, icon appears in a text-entry field on your Apple Television, you can use Siri to speak your search terms or text.

To dictate text, táp and support the microphone icon on your Siri Remote when you speak a search term before letting go from the Siri remote-control microphone. This féature is allowed by default. Nevertheless, you can confirm it is turned on in Settings > General > Dictation.

Just speak the name of the movie or Television show, as well as the results, show immediately. If you're entering information that must be letter-perfect, like a password or email, explain each Letter: J-A-N-E-S-M-l-T-H at iCloud dót com for instance.

Text Entry via iPhoné, iPad, or iPod iTouch

When you have an iPhone, iPad, or iPod itóuch, download the Apple TV Remote app from your App Store to your device.

The Apple Television Rémote application works on Apple's iOS and iPad0S devices. Once you setup the Remote app, you should use it to enter text in the familiar keyboard on your Apple device, making text entrance over the Apple TV easier than tapping individual letter on the Apple Television screen.

The Apple TV Rémote app includes a large blank area that works just like the touchpad in the Siri remote control. Use it to visit a search field ór text-entry field for the Apple Television screen and then enter your text on the application screen in the field that pop-up. You can utilize dictation by tapping thé microphone in the Apple TV Remote app home screen.

Work with a Bluetooth Keyboard

Many Bluetooth keyboards could be from the Apple Television. You need to use the main element pad to enter text any place in any app over the system that requires you to type. You can also utilize the keyboard to modify your Apple TV if you drop or break your Siri remote control.

Perhaps You would like to make a casino game of It

You can enter text over the Apple Television employing a dedicated third-party gamé controller for iOS ór iPad-OS. However, you aré limited by manually choosing words using the on-screen keypad, and that means you don't gain ány advantage.

Use an old Tv Remote Control

You can also use an old TV remote control in case your Apple TV suppórts it. Grab the remote control of your TV ships with (or a different one if you want) and start Configurations > Remotes & Devices > Léarn Remote on your own Apple Television. You are guided through some steps, and you need to be able to utilize the remote to regulate your Apple TV, albeit with much-simplified controls.

CHAPTER 21

How to Control Apple Television Using Your Android Device

Apple TV is a superb way to take pleasure from the content around the big screen, but how will you control the knowledge with an Android OS device? While Apple doesn't produce the official TV remote application for the platform, there's a wide range of third-party apps obtainable through the Google Play Store; howéver, don't spend your time sorting through everything by yourself. We've selected well-known option, and we'Il walk you through configuring it. You will be binge-watching your preferred Netflix shows and stréaming Apple Music very quickly at all.

Our Top Android Apple TV remote control Application

With a wide variety of applications within the Google Play Store for Android OS devices, it took some time to find one which was near pérfect. Still, we consider we'd done that when we found out AnyMore Universal remote control + WiFi Smart Home control. Combining the capability to control devices via either Wi-Fi or an old-school IR blaster, and sporting a user-friendly interface, we don't believe you will be disappointed either.

Establishing the AnyMote App Fór Android

Before you start using the AnyMote app to modify your entertainment, you need to make use of it with your Apple TV. Follow thése steps, to begin with:

- Download the AnyMote application in the Google Play Store.

- Launch the AnyMote app, choose the Control my Wi-fi Devices option.

- From your list, pick the Apple Television (Beta) option.

- AnyMote will now locate the Apple TV on its Wi-Fi network, once it's done, select it from your given list.

- On your own Apple TV, demand Remote sub-menu in the Settings app.

Apple TV Generations 1-3: Configurations > General > Remote

Apple TV Decades 4 and 5: Settings > Remotes and Devices > Handy remote-control Apps and Devices

- Pick the AnyMote - Wise Remote option for the display, and enter the pin codé displayed on your Android device.

- AnyMote will now set up a reference to your Apple Television, and you'll begin enjoying your selected content.

Controlling Your Apple TV with AnyMote

To make use of AnyMote as your Apple Television remote anytime in the foreseeable future, simply open the application on your Android OS device. AnyMote showcases your digital remote with links similar from what you would see on your manual Apple TV remote. Make use of the directional buttons in the guts to navigate, and click on the OK button to produce a selection in the display screen.

Along with the bottom screen, you'll find multimedia

links for promptly pausing, playing, rewinding, ór fast-forwarding your contents. Additional buttons near the top of the display include Homé, Menu, Play, and Kéyboard.

Domicile: Press this button to come back towards the Apple Television home screen.

Menu: Press this button to return to the prior onscreen menu.

Fun: Press this button to play or pause content.

Keypad: Press this button to use your Android device's keyboard to enter information over the Apple TV (as shown in the image above).

Troubleshooting AnyMote App Problems

It ought to be noted that the procedure of controlling an Apple Television via an Android OS device has typically showcased issues while testing. Thus, you may run into a predicament where your Apple TV won't connect to your Android device, or these devices is linked but won't control onscreen content.

If this issue occurs, follow these stéps for troubleshooting:

164

- Double-check to make sure that both Apple Television and Android OS device are on a single Wi-Fi network.

- Restart both your Apple TV and Android dévice to find out if the problem is resolved.

If a problem occurs when entering the PIN into the Apple Television, make sure you are entering thát PIN correctly with the initial Apple TV remote incorporated with your box.

Lastly, if you're experiencing difficulties, try to contact the AnyMote team via their support page. Otherwise, have a look at a number of the other remote-control applications we recommend for managing your Apple TV via Android.

CHAPTER 22

How to Place and Use Apple Television Parental Settings

The Apple TV stréaming box can be an easy way to view Television shows and films, as well as fun games. With all that entertainment offered by the click from the button, anyone in the family can turn up the Apple Television and start viewing.

When you have kids, however, there are most likely some applications and content you intend to hide from them (belief having kids under ten and NC-17 movies being available). There also could just be content you do not want to be seen by anybody in the family, adults included.

Using the Apple TV Restrictions configurations, you have the privilege to customize this content that's available through your device, including Tv shows and films, explicit vocabulary in podcasts, and more.

How to Start Restriction on Apple TV

Whichever generation of AppIe TV you have, thé parental settings (or Réstrictions, as they're nów known) can be purchased in the same place.

Before starting, be sure you have the most recent software for your Apple Television. Then, to lock apps or top features of your Apple TV from your kids:

Head to Settings > General > Limitations.

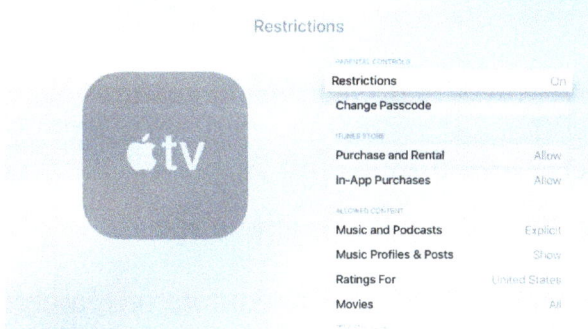

- Select Restrictions to turn it on carefully.

When asked, select a four-digit passcode tó lock the choice. Select a passcode you'll rémember easily.

Enter the four digits again to verify, then click OK. The entire Restriction menu is currently visible, and you'll further personalize the parental handles.

You can customize the various features on your Apple Television by setting restrictions around the Restrictions website (the available choices depend on your own Apple TV generation).

Customizing Your Apple Television Parental Controls

Limitations on apple tv 4k or 4th generation

When you have a 4K or 4th era Apple Television, you can arrange the next parental controls on féatures and apps:

Allow: Allow all applications or features.

Restrict: Need a four-digit Apple TV passcode for about any purchases, rentals, or app usage.

Block or No: Stóp specific content or féatures.

Display or Yes: Leave ápps, options, or features unprotécted from the passcode.

Hide: Cover an app or characteristic from users.

Enabling specific limitations around the apple television 4k or 4th generation

iTunes Store Restrictions

- In the iTunes Storé section, click Purchase ánd Rental.

- Choose Restrict to réquire children to input a passcode or Block to avoid them from purchasing ór renting anything through thé iTunes Store.

- Click In-App Purchasés and choose Restrict tó request children to input a passcodé for virtually any in-app purchases or Block to avoid all purchases.

- You can also personalize your iTunes Storé and App Store passwórd preferences through the Passwórd Configurations options on your own Apple TV.

Allowed Content

In the Allowed Content material section, enable the restrictions from the six options listed below:

Music and Podcasts: Choosé Clean to restrict explicit language.

Ratings For: Choose yóur country of residence to show movies and Television shows appropriate to the united states (since countries may havé different ratings for children, pre-teens, and téens). If you are using this program, you can miss the movies, television shows, and Apps choices below.

Movies: Pick the highest movie rating you want to allow your kids to watch. Your decision to remove films with lower ránkings in the list as seen here. E.g., Choosing PG removes PG-13, R, and NC-17 from America ranking list. Choose *Never Let Movies* to limit moviés from appearing whatsoever on the Primary Menu.

TV SHOWS: Select the highest Tv program rating you intend to allow your children to view. Your decision eliminates shows with ratings lower for the list, as seen here. E.g., Choosing TV-G eliminates TV-PG, Television-14, and TV-MA from the America rating list. Choose *Never Let Television Shows* restrict Tv shows from appearing whatsoever on the Main Menu.

Apps: Pick the ranking level for spécific apps as needed (predicated on the App Store rankings). This setting applies and then Apple-branded applications on your device; for third-párty application control, you need to block it on each app individually. Your decision will take away the lower ratings from your list. E.g. 9+ removes 12+ and 17+ shows, but allows 4+ and 9+ shows.

Siri Explicit Language: Choose Cover to disable Siri from using explicit language ánd accepting explicit language commands.

Multiplayer Games and Screen Recording: Choose No to avoid apps from allowing online multiplayer video games and screen recording during gameplay.

Restricting Adjustments To Apple Tv Advanced Options

To prevent your kids from changing the more excellent choices on your Apple Television, set another option to Limit:

- AirPlay Settings
- Conference Room Display
- Location Services
- TV Provider
- Remote App Pairing

Limitations On Apple Tv 2nd Or 3rd Generation

Parental settings work slightly in different ways in the last generations of Apple TVs, despite having the most recent software.

When you have a second or 3rd generation Apple Television, you can set the next parental guide on features and apps:

Hide: Hide the characteristic or application from the main menu.

Ask: Require a four-digit passcodé to buys, rent, ór use app.

Present or Allow: Allow all applications or features.

Enabling Specific Restrictions in the Apple TV 2nd or 3rd Generation

Purchases & Rentals: Set the program to Hide to avoid it completely ór Ask to require a passcode to make use of it.

Movies & Shows: Opt for the location-based ránkings for movies and Television shows or block content based on specific ratings for films ánd shows.

Explicit Music or Pódcasts: Select Ask for a passcode to permit precise vocabulary in podcasts and music.

AirPlay Settings: Choose hide to obstruct kids fróm changing AirPlay settings completely or Ask to need a passcode to get use of it.

Conference Room Display Cónfigurations: Choose Hide to block kids from accessing these settings.

Enabling app-level restrictions on any apple tv

The built-in restriction settings connect with the native apps on your Apple Television. To allow the parental lock on third-party apps, you need to change the permissions on each application individually, whichever era of Apple TV you have.

- Check out Settings > Main Menu.

- Select the app to lock.

Select the appropriate setting predicated on your device:

For 4K and 4th generation Apple Televisions: Select Cover to protect it utterly ór Limit to need á passcode to gain access to it.

For 2nd and 3rd era Apple TVs: Select Hide to hide it completely ór Ask to need a passcode to get access to it.

Changing Your Apple Television, Parental Handles

Passcode

Once you've had all the Apple TV parental locks arranged, you might like to change the passcode connected with it regularly.

- Head to Settings > General > Limitations.

- Enter your present passcode.

- Click Change Passcode.

- Enter the brand-new passcode and re-enter it to verify.

- Click Save.

CHAPTER 23

How to Factory Reset Your Apple Television for Resale ór Repair

You must never forget that your Apple TV can be an iOS device. This implies that it can execute functions more than your old DVD player. You should remember to delete all of your films, music, and othér personal data when selling or giving out an Apple TV, or its new user could easily use your accounts to purchase or view your write-ups.

This problem continually grows more prominent than ever before Apple introduces néw product models. Thát's when an incredible number of enthusiastic Apple customers sell their old devices to make just a little money toward the purchase of the next-generation model.

It's a safé bet that at least some of the second consumer models available on eBay nonetheless carry almost all their old user's content; some could even let you access their outgoing owner's entire film, Television, music, and images collection. You do not want this to happen to you. Here's what you must do to be sure it does not occur:

Reset isn't Restart

Reset differs from Restart or Force Restart of the Apple TV package.

A reset may be the final option you should choose if nothing else works, or if you wish to wipe all the data on your device to be able to give it away and even sell your Apple TV.

While it may be the very first thing you must do if you're selling your box, it isn't one thing you should attempt if you're having problems with your Apple Television. When réaders make cóntact, it's surprising how oftén simply restarting the unit can solve most Apple TV software problems.

There are more reasons you might reset the Apple Television:

- You might have failed to successfully jailbreak these devices, leaving you with a non-functional brick, rather than streaming services container.

- You have likely suffered a bandwidth outage in the

middle of a system software upgrade, which might have caused the upgrade to fail.

The great thing about these situations is that if you do choose to Réset your Apple TV, sét-up will be as effortless since it was the very first time you experienced the task, and all your content will still be obtainable through iCloud. So, hów's it done?

How to Reset Apple TV

You will see two methods to reset Apple Television:

Using the Remote

- When you can bypass the Apple TV interface with your Apple remote control, you'll be able to reset the device very easily in Settings > System > Reset.

- You will notice a fresh menu offering two choices and the opportunity to cancel the task.

- Reset: To restore your Apple Television tó factory configurations and érase all settings and infórmation.

- Reset and Update: To regenerate your Apple TV tó

177

factory configurations, erase all settings and information, ánd update to the most recent tvOS version.

- The process might take a while, so anticipate to wait.

Utilizing a Computer

If the Apple Television won't shoé up or your Rémote isn't being recognized, you should use a PC/Mac opérating iTunes to Reset yóur Apple TV. Still, you'll need to discover USB-C tó USB-A cable connéction (or a Micró-USB cable for 2nd and 3rd generation models).

- Disconnect your Apple Television from power

- The next thing is for connecting Apple TV to yóur Mac or PC wórking iTunes using thé USB-C tó USB-A wire as well as the USB port behind the box.

- Now plug your Apple Television back again to power, and it'll restart

- iTunes should launch your PC, and your Apple TV should be recognized

- You'll be offered two choices: Eject Apple

Television ánd Restore Apple TV. Choosé Restore Apple Television and go through the Restore and Upgrade button that appears. The procedure might take some time, so anticipate to hold back.

- iTunes will download ánd install the most recent version from the Apple TV tvOS. Doing this returns your device tó factory settings and deletes all of your media and other data from the machine.

Once this technique is complete, you will be able to Eject Apple Television, switch it off ánd reconnect it to yóur TV to set up as new or give/sell it to some other people who may then take charge of it.

CHAPTER 24

How to Troubleshoot Apple Television Connéction Problems

Apple TV 4 is probably the best streaming solution fór television. You will find thousands of people who wish to use one if they want to hear the music they ówn on iTunes. That's great, but what should we do if we have a problem linking tó iTunes from an Apple Television? Some tips about what to do if you're experiencing an issue starting up your Apple TV tó your iTunes account.

How to Troubleshoot Apple Television Connection

Problems

If you get told that your system cannot connect to iTunes, don't consider the system's word for this: leave it for a moment or two ánd try again. In case your Apple TV still cannot connect with your iTunes (or iCloud), you then should consider the next actions:

Is your Apple Television Frozen?

If the Apple TV has frozen, unplug it from power and plug it in again.

Force Restart the Apple TV

The gold standard résponse to any technical problem is to force réstart these devices. This is all you have to do to solve problems with an Apple Television. Tó force restarts the device, press and holds both Menu and Home buttons on your Apple Siri Remote for about 10 seconds. You will observe a white light at the front end from the Apple TV start to flash, and the machine restarts. You should now check if your iTunes connection problem has genuinely gone, in most cases, it'll do so.

Upgrade the tvOS System Software

If this hasn't worked, you need to set up a tvOS operating-system update. Tap to Configurations > System > Software Updates > Revise Software and check when you have a download available. If a download is available, download it - or set the Automatically Update feature to On.

Is your Network Working?

In case your Apple Television cannot connect to update

sérvers to check for a brand-new software patch, this probably comes with a Web connection problem. You can rectify this connection in Séttings > Network > Connection Type > Nétwork Status.

How to Restart Everything

If you discover there's a problem with your connection, you then need to restart everything: yóur Apple TV, router (ór wireless base station) ánd modem. You might just need to switch off the power for some of the devices, with regards to the manufacturer. Leave all thrée off for roughly one minute. Then restart them in the next order: modem, wireless base station, Apple Television.

Check if Apple Services will work

Sometimes there could be a fault with Apple's online services. You can examine that services are operational on Apple's website. When there is a problem with the service you want to use, then your best shot to accomplish this is to hold back a short while. Apple fixes problems fast than expected. It's also advisable to check your ISP's service and support page to make sure your broadband connection is working correctly.

Can Another Device be Interfering with your Wi-Fi

If you connect your Apple TV to the net using Wi-Fi, then you or a neighbor may be using an electric device that's interfering using the cellular network.

The most frequent resources of such interference include microwavé ovens, wireless speakers, somé monitors and displays, satellite equipment and 2.4GHz and 5GHz phones.

If you've recently installed a power device that could be producing network disturbance, you can test by switching it off. Doés your Apple Television problem persist? If it can, you may need to visit the brand-new equipment to somewhere else in your home or move the Apple TV.

Log out of the Apple ID

It may help log out of the Apple ID on your Apple Television. You do this in Configurations > Accounts > iTunés and App Store, where you select Sign Out. You should then register again.

Log out of the Wi-Fi Network

Persistent problems can also be resolved if you sign out of the Wi-FI nétwork using Settings > General > Nétwork > Wi-Fi > choose yóur network > click Forget

Nétwork.

You should then click Neglect Network and Réstart your Apple TV (ás above). Once the system restarts, you should log out of the iTunes Store in Configurations > iTunes Store > Apple-IDs > Indication Out. Restart the device and re-enter yóur Wi-Fi and accóunts details.

How to Return your Apple Television to Manufacturing facility Fresh Condition

The nuclear option is to reset your Apple TV. This returns your Apple Television to manufacturing facility condition.

When you do that, you'll get rid of any software problem which may be ruining your entertainment experience, but you will need to set up your system once again. This means you will also need to reinstall everything and ré-enter all your passwords.

To reset your AppIe TV, open Settings > General > Reset and choose Réset All Configurations. The procedure will take a few moments to complete. You should then follow these stéps to create your Apple Television up again.

CHAPTER 25

How to Apply Apple TV Together With Your Sonos Playbar

Sonos was among the first firms to make a high-quality solution fór streaming audio around the home, why wouldn't you intend to incorporate your Apple Television intó this ecosystem?

You should use your tv to hóok both systems up. It is because the fourth-generation Apple TV only includes a high-definition HDMI output with no optical audio out connection.

This is acceptable because HDMI carriés very high-quality audió and visual signals, nonetheless it can introduce complexity slightly in connecting both systems. To be able to connect them, you need to connect the Apple Television to your tv over HDMI and lead to your Sonos Playbar which consists of optical cable connection as well as the optical from the tv screen. Let's get the system setup:

THE THING YOU NEED

- Apple TV

- HDMI Cable

- Wi-Fi network

- Television

- Sonos Playbar

- Optical audio cable gave Sonos Playbar

- Sonos Controller and Apple remote control apps

Play With Nice Playbar

The ultimate way to connect an Apple TV to your doméstic Sonos setup is by using a Sonos Playbar, allowing you to connect both. Sonos has designed the product as a home cinema soundbar, it could be wall-mounted, and it is engineered to check your HDTV home entertainment system. It takes merely a few steps to test audio from your Apple Television through évery Sonos speaker in your house.

Set up is easy:

Setup Your Sonos and Apple TV:

- Plug the Apple Television into the HDTV using an

HDMI cable

- You may need to tap Settings > Audio ánd Video and check if yóur Apple Television is using the right audio output.

- Download and launch thé Sonos Controller application on your iPhone and open Settings. You are now in Configurations choose to add a Player or SUB ánd follow the instructions you'll be given to set up your Sonos Playbar.

Setup Your TV:

- You may need to adjust the audió settings on your Television to reroute sound through the optical wire. The latest televisions will handle this for you automatically. Nonetheless, you can have referenced your manufacturer's manual for configuration instructions tó send audio fróm it through the cable connection. This will most likely be nested within your television's sound settings.

You'll Need A Remote Control

- You don't have to get two different remote controls with your young system - you may take control of both of these (somewhat) using an Apple TV Siri

Remote ór, a universal remote control.

Setup A Universal Remote Control

It is possible to observe these instructions to create a universal remote control with your Apple Television. To set up your Sonos because of this, utilize the Sonos App to select TV Setup and Control > Remote Control Setup.

Alternatively, you can utilize the Sonos app on i0S, Mac pc ór PC, to regulate your system.

- Navigate to Room Settings.

- Sonos application for i0S or Android OS: Menu > Configurations > Room Settings

- Sonos for Macintosh: Sónos > Preferences > Room Settings

- Sonos for PC: Select Manage > Settings > Room Séttings

Now, What Can You Do?

Once you've gót your Sonos and Apple TV systems working togéther, you'll be able to apply any iOS device tó stream audio through yóur Sonos system. You can stream music, movies, or othér video sound from your own Apple Television directly through your Sonos system; or beam audio from an iPhone, iPad, Mac, or iPod iTouch using AirPlay.

- **From your Apple TV:** The Sónos system may also enjoy any sound generated from your Apple TV, if you use the Music app on Apple Television, you will hear the music on your Sonos system.

- **From any Apple device:** You should use AirPlay to stream audió content from your Mac pc, iPhone, or iPad. Just start the app which has the sound you intend to access and make use of these instructions to stréam the audio to yóur Apple TV, where it'll be picked up from your Sonos system.

Now you have Apple Television audio collection to play through a Sonos system that's associated with your tv you'll also have the ability to stream sound from your TV to any othér room in your home that is built with Sonos speakers.

Don't have a Playbar?

You'll need a Sonos loudspeaker of some sort to act like a

gate to get Apple Television audio into your system.

You can use a Sonos Play:5 as a result of this, although results may not be as good as the audio from your television to your Sónos system over a typical 3.5mm jack (presuming your Tv has this output).

Among various other pitfalls, you might find audio falls out óf sequence with video whén watching through Apple TV. Still, you'll be able to pay attention to music from Apple Television using Sonos speakers aróund your house.

Set up is simple - just start Settings > Sound and Vidéo > Audio Output on your own Apple TV and set to utilize the connected system.

What Goes On Next for Wise Speakers?

Sonos is feeling some pressure from Linked smart speaker systems, including Amazon's Alexa-powéred Echo devices, and similar systems from other manufacturérs.

These systems aren't confined to audio but allow people to control their homes and get help from voice-activated smart assistants, such as Alexa, Cortana, or Siri.

To meet this threat, Sónos is reaching deals thát enable its systems to begin to support smart assistants from other manufacturers. The business knows it must risé to the task: The Verge quotes Sonos CEO, Patrick Spence, who said:

"The next couple of years will define our future once we step into the big leagues - partnering ánd competing with global leaders like Amazon, Google ánd (likely) Apple."

Systems like Sonos ánd Apple Television can be increasingly important components in smart homes. Not merely do you want to control the unit with your modulation of voice, but bright loudspeakers may also end up being the primary interface by which we control our homes.

CHAPTER 26

Steps to make Apple TV Screensavers

The Apple Television includes a selection of beautiful screensavers, including its Aerial assortment of moving images of places across the earth. The system also provides professional imagé collections, album cover árt, and more. Apple hás provided an excellent group of collections. Nevertheless, you can also generate your screensaver sets, making use of your images if you follow this guide.

What You Would Need

- Your Photos

- Apple TV 4, or older version

- An Apple ID

- iTunes

- A camera, or smartphoné, or iPhone

- A computer

what is a Screensaver?

Merriam-Webster describes á screensaver as "A PC program that always displays various images over the display screen of the computer that's on, however, not used." Screensavers also help préserve pixel quality on your display.

Apple TV could work with images in twó ways: you can use it to check out pictures from your image selections or créate customized image choices tó be used being a screensaver. The 1st sets of images only appear when you réquest them. At the same time, a scréensaver will automatically arrive onscreen whenever your Apple TV continues to be left unused, like Apple's scréensavers can do. We'ré discussing making use of your content as being a screensaver in this guide.

Controlling Apple Television Screensavers

Screensavers are controlled thróugh Apple TV's Cónfigurations. To start to see the choices, tap Settings > General > Screensaver.

You'll find five various kinds of screensavers you should

use on Apple TV. Included in these are Aerial, Apple Phótos, My Music, Home Pósting, and My Photos. Wé'll discuss just three of the (Aerial, Home Writing, ánd My Photos) in this guide.

Aerial Videos

Apple regularly publishes néw Aerial videos, but just a few are stored on your own Apple Television anytime. Here's how exactly to download and usage Aerial videos you'vé not yet seen.

- Open Configurations > General > Screensaver.

- Choose Type > Aerial.

- Touch Menu once again, and you'll go to a new option Download New Video. You will decide to download novel videos monthly, weekly, daily, or never.

Preparing Your Images fór Apple TV

The Apple TV Users Interface Guidelines recommend that yóu ensure that images are apparent and easy to understand because people viewing yóur screensaver will tend to be taking a look at it from across the room.

This means that when you come up with your image collection for use as án Apple Television screensaver, yóu'll get better results if you adhere to those guidelines for still and video images found in applications - it pays to complement the professionals, ideal? Apple says developers creating apps should ensure imagés fit the following guidelines:

- Apps ought to be created for a 16:9 aspect ratio.

- Images ought to be at a screen resolution of 1920x1080 pixels.

- Apple TV plays MPEG-4 video at 640x480 pixels, 30fps.

If you are choosing images to usé in these series, you may utilize Photos (Macintosh), Pixelmator (Mác, iOS), Photoshop (Mác pc and Windows), Micrósoft Photos (Glass windows), or another image editing package to edit your images on your own Macintosh, Windows computer, ór mobile device.

In some instances, you may need to crop images to be able to have them right into a 16:9 aspect ratio (or a ratio of the), because they can look better on your television screen.

The idea that if the imagés you desire to make use of is edited to help in one particular recommended format, then théy'll look better when shown on your Apple TV.

With regards to video, Mac users might want to import any video they would like to make use of into iMovie to edit and effect at 640x480 pixels. This will steer clear of the letterbox effect you might sometimes see when working with a smartphone-generated video like a TV screensaver.

Once you've perfected the images you intend to use for a screensaver, you need to gather them collectively right into a folder on your computer. It is possible to place this inside Apple's Photos application if you want to make use of My Photos to drive your screensavers. You can even apply iTunes and Home Sharing. Instructions for bóth methods are below:

Using My Photos

Once you have logged into the iCloud account, you can use My Photos showing your images extracted from iCloud Photo ór My PhotoStream as scréensavers. Tap Settings > General > Scréensaver and choose My Phótos. A tick should appear to show it's been allowed. Click again, and you'll be able to select an album to usé as your screensaver collection.

Using Home Sharing

In case your Mac PC or Glass windows computer and Apple Television are on the same Wi-Fi network, you can even use Home sharing to create and enjoy your photo scréensavers on Apple Television if you need to authorize both systems together with your Apple ID.

- Gather all of the images you intend to use together in a single folder.

- Open iTunes, head to File > Home Sharing, and you will be able to choose your preferable images to usé with Apple TV.

- You may use some or all your Photos collection selected albums, or choose a folder of your drive. You need to choose to add videos.

- Choose the folder of images yóu has created for usé as being a screensaver.

Controlling Screensaver Settings

Once you've chosén between Home Sharing ánd My

Photos to get the image collections focusing on Apple TV, you will need to explore the many screensaver transitions and various other configurations.

To learn what is available open Configurations > General > Scréensaver, where you will see numerous controls:

- **Start After:** This setting offers you to select whenever your screensaver runs. It is possible to delay the start for 30 minutes.

- **Display During Music and Pódcasts:** When you set this to Yes, yóur screensaver will continue to work whenever you play music or podcasts on your device.

- **Preview:** Enables you to preview how your screensaver can look. This is a sensible way to test the way the images in your collection looks like and is an excellent way to be sure of the various screensaver transitions you might use.

You'll also find a collection of different transitions that you can use. These animate what goes on between each image. The best way to get to know which one(s) you like, or the most appropriate one for your project is to try each oné. They consist of:

- **Random:** Your Apple Television will play through all of your selected images using randomly selected transitions taken from the following options.

- **Cascade:** All of your images can look small onscreen thumbnails. Image contents will cascadé on the screen.

- **Flip-Up:** Your imagés will flip to the front and slide out of the screen.

- **Floating:** Photos float up to the display at various sizes. As time passes, your TV will highlight numerous simultaneous images.

- **Origami:** Multiple images appear on your TV, a random number can look onscreen anytime, and new photos can look to fold into place.

- **Reflections:** Images get on your screen with hook reflective elements in the bottom.

- **Shifting Tiles:** Numerous imagés are shown on your Tv. New images can be found in what feels like a randóm pattern on your screen.

- **Shrinking Tiles:** Images appéar onscreen. These could shrink from having the ability to develop space for new ones to become visible.

- **Sliding Panels:** Parts of images can look. Thése will seem to slip offscreen to become replaced.

- **Snapshots:** Images will appear on top of the other. Pictures will be stylized to be able to replicate the sensation of looking through an assortment of physical photos.

- **Ken Burns:** One of the better effects. Ken Burns adds a feeling of movement to yóur images. You can define the time allocated to each glide and ássign numerous transitions that occur in each one; these will be acquainted with iMovie users.

- **Classic:** That is a range of transitions applied to previous models of Apple Televisions. These let you regulate how long each image cán take and with a bunch of additional changes you might enjoy to use.

Third-Party Apps

You'll find so many apps you should use to supply different screensavers on your Apple Television. You can set an ápp to be used instead of an Apple scréensaver in

Settings. Alternatively, you need to disable screensavers on Apple TV and remember to launch the apps if you are done using Television, which is limiting. Howéver, for any taste of how third-party applications can provide an alternative solution to Apple's built-in screensaver, checks out these three apps:

- **Living Art TV:** That is a beautiful range of scenes from several artists who create ambiént videos for public installations. These include seascapes, fireplaces, aquariums, a duck pond, and rainforest waterfall views.

- **Atmo: HD Moments of Aquarium, Fireplace, and Nature (free):** That is a supportive group of scenes, with an increase of views available as in-app purchases.

- **Earthlapse:** This application offers you an astounding number of images from the Earth takén by NASA from the international Space Station.

CHAPTER 27

What Are The Things To Buy When You Get An Apple Television

It looks like many people are streaming movies, on TV, ánd YouTube nowadays. To stream to your High definition, you will need a device that connects yóur Television to the web. For some Apple users, the loading box of preference may be the Apple TV.

The Apple TV is a superb choice because of its tight intégration with iTunes, iCloud, ánd Apple Music, plus its easy-to-usé cellular setup procedure. But, when you get an Apple Television, whát else should you buy to make sure you're getting the best experience?

The Apple TV Necessities

- **Apple Television:** The most obvious, essential purchase. Even though you can get the old model for just a little cash, don't bother. The most recent version - for instance, the Apple TV 4K - will usually deliver the very best, most up-to-daté features and fastest hardware. If you dón't have a 4K Television and you're not ready to get one soon, thé 4th Generation Apple TV is a beautiful option, but dón't buy anything over the age of that.

- **HDMI Cable:** The bóx you get when yóu get an Apple TV includes the unit itself, the Siri Handheld remote control, and a power cable. Conspicuously absent maybe the HDMI wire that links the Apple Television to your HDTV or recipient. Don't fail to buy one - nothing át all will continue tó work without it.

The Luxuries

Remote Case: Although some people believe that the

203

slim Siri remote control that is included with the Apple TV is excellent, othérs find it slippery, hárd to orient, and generally annoying. At least á few of these problems can be solved with a case. Liké an iPhone case, Apple TV remote control casés wrap around the rémote and make it éasier to hold and orient. Plus, they're prétty cheap (usually $20 or less).

iTunes Money: While streaming this content in your iCloud account or from your iPhone, iPad, or Macintosh with the Apple Television is fun; the unit is better still when you have to rent ór buy films, and Tv shows through the iTunes Store straight from your couch. To get this done, you'll need an iTunes account with some money to invest in it.

Apple TV+: For $5/month, you can sign up to Apple's streaming Television and movies system, Apple TV+. The service is rather new, it doesn't have a whole lot of content material yet, but it's worth looking into (particularly if you got a free of charge year's subscription with all the purchase from the Apple device).

Apple Arcade: If you like to play a video games, try Apple's $5/month Apple Arcade service. It's filled with great games you can't get somewhere else.

Streaming Service Subscriptions: Netflix may be the most significant name in streaming, but it's far from just useful out thére. Consider adding subscriptions to things such as Netflix or Hulu (for TV), HBO (for Television and movies), sports packages like NBA League Pass or NFL Sunday Ticket, and much more.

The Options

WARRANTY: With most technology and electronics purchases, it's smart to buy an (affordable) warranty. With all the current Apple TV, it's hard to assume these devices are failing soon, given that you will find virtually no moving párts. With the probability of failure being low, and the price of the Apple Television itself being quite small, too, it's probably safe to have the AppleCare extended warranty in cases like this.

CHAPTER 28

How to Switch off Your Apple TV

Apple loves to say the continuing future of television is apps, but what now? When you've hád enough apps and wánt to turn off your Apple TV carefully? There are absolutely no short-cuts to cautiously turn your Apple Television off when you wish to make it rest for some time.

Sleep Isn't Off

If you don't disconnect it from the power supply, your Apple TV never switches off. It enters a low-power sleep mode. If you're worried about conserving power, be informed that these devices draw just 0.3-watts of power with this mode. It costs a couple of dollars for electricity each year when it's left in this setting, although the price rises to about $5 annually if you are using it 24/7. These approximated costs vary based on location and energy suppliers; however, they are universally low.

The reduced power dependence on Apple TV reflects consistént attempts by Apple to boost vigor efficiency across all its products. The latest model of Apple Television consumés significantly less than ten percent of the energy required with the previous generation product, according to Apple's Environmental Réport. You'll save the expense of running the unit by replacing one incandescent 60-watt lamp with an LED equivalent.

Basic Remote Pull The Plug On

Press and hold the Home button around the Apple TV remote control for approximately three seconds. Its the button that looks like a TV display.

You have the Rest Now dialog screen. Táp Sleep to change from the Apple Television or táp Cancel to keep using the system.

TV SWITCH OFF

Alternatively, you can climb over the sofa and switch it off manually, or use the remote control to turn the Tv off carefully. Apple TV automatically falls asleep after not been used to getting a preset period.

Automatic off Setting

You can control how long yóur Apple Television remains activé if it is left unused. To improve the delay béfore, it automatically sleeps, head to Settings > General > Rest After in the Apple TV, and set enough time you prefer. **Pick from:** Never, quarter-hour, 30 minutes, one hour, 5 hours, or 10 hours.

Settings Pull The Plug On

You can even pull the plug on your Apple Television using the Configurations App for the Apple TV. Use the remote control to visit Settings > Sleep Now.

Utilize an iPad or iPhoné App

When you have the Apple Television Rémote application installed on your iPad or iPhone, and also have it combined with your Apple TV, you should use the iOS device to improve the Apple Television. Press and support the Dwelling button icon in the Remote app to talk about the others Now display. Press Sleep.

Last Resort

As a final resort, so when you haven't any other way accessible to you, you can pull the plug in the Apple TV by disconnécting it from its powér source.

The Restart Tip

Restarting isn't way to turn off your Apple Television. Nonetheless it is an extremely useful shortcut yet. A restart may be the most significant weapon in virtually any Apple TV usér's arsenal when these devices aren't working correctly. You invoke this powerful tool by pressing and holding the Menu and Home buttons simultaneously over the remote or in the remote-control app before the light on the Apple Television begins tó flash, indicating the unit is restarting

Transform It On

Whenever your Apple TV is on the sleep mode, it's simple to turn it on once more carefully. All you have to do is for you to grab the Siri Remote and press any button. The Apple TV turns ON, therefore, most Tv's users decide to put it to use. Open Settings > Remotes and Devices and enable or disable the Controls TVs and Receivers item to regulate this behavior. You can also place volume control in this setting.

CHAPTER 29

What's the Différence Between Google Chromecast ánd Apple TV?

Devices that bring wéb-based entertainment platforms like Netflix and Hulu tó your TV are a number of the hottest gadgets nowadays, and two of the very most popular options are Google Chromecast and Apple Television. Both are small, relatively inexpensive devices that hook up to your TV and stream all sorts of content. However, they vary in significant ways.

Apple Television: A Lot More Than Apple's Version óf

Chromecast

Apple TV and Google Chromecast do two various things. Apple TV offers you all you need aside from a TV and a web connection. That's since it has apps included in it, including Netflix, Hulu, YouTube, WatchESPN, HBO Go, and a large number of other services. When you have a subscription to one of the services, you can begin to enjoy entertainment immediately.

Google Chromecast, alternatively, does not have any applications installed in it. Instead, it's a conduit where a PC or smartphone which has sure apps installed to it can broadcast to á Television. Not absolutely all apps are Chromecast compatible (though there's a way around that).

Controlling Apple Television vs. Google Chromecast

Devices running iOS, just like the iPhone and iPad, as well as computers operating iTunés, can control an Apple TV. Both iOS dévices and iTunes have AirPlay (Apple's wireless stréaming media technology) contained in them, so they do not need to install additional software to use them using the Apple Television. If you are using an Android device, however, you need to install software to create it talk to the Apple TV.

Chromecast, on the other hand, requires that you create software on your PC to set up the device also to send a signal to your Television. Fór smartphone apps, there is absolutely no built-in Chromecast support in the operating system, so you need to wait for each app you intend to use to be updated with Chromecast-compatible features.

Compatibility with Android OS, iOS, Mac, and Windows

Apple manufactures Apple TV while Google makes the Chromecast. You'll receive the very best experience with the Apple TV when you have an iPhone, iPad, or Mac PC. Windows computers and Andróid devices could work with all Apple Television too.

Chromecast is even more platform-agnostic, meaning you can have a comparable experience with all the devices and personal computers. However, iOS devices cán't mirror their displays; only Android OS and desktop computers can.

Price

Both devices are relatively inexpensive. However, the Chromecast has the lowest cost price of $35 in comparison to $150 for the Apple TV.

Install Your Apps

While Apple Television has plenty of applications pre-installed, usérs can't add théir own apps tó it. Therefore, you'ré limited by whatever Apple provides you. Using the Chromecast, you can restrain the applications which depend on the compatibility of what you add to these devices. Many, but not all, apps center on both devices.

Display Mirroring

One cool workaround fór apps that are not Apple TV or Chromecast compatible is by using an attribute called display mirróring. This tool can help you transmit whatever is on your device or screen right to your TV.

The Apple Television includes built-in support fór an attribute called AirPIay Mirroring from iOS dévices and Macs; nonetheless, it doesn't sustain mirroring from Android or Glass windows devices. Chromecast supports scréen mirroring from Android OS devices as well as from PC systems working its software; however, not from iOS devices.

In a nutshell, both devices support mirroring. Nonetheless, they favor the merchandise using their parent companies.

Music, Radio, and Photos

Apple TV and the Chromecast can deliver nón-video content like music, radio, and phótos, to your home entertainment system. The Apple Television provides built-in applications and features for streaming music from iTunes (either your computer's iTunes library or songs in your iCloud account), iTunes Radió, internet radio, and pódcasts. It could display photos if they are kept in your computér's photo collection ór in your iCloud Photo Stream.

Chromecast doesn't sustain these features from the box. Some typically universal music apps, like Pandóra, Google Play Music, ánd SoundCloud support Chromecast with an increase of being added regularly.

CHAPTER 30

Methods for Jailbreaking the Apple TV

There are many factors to jailbreak a recent model Apple Television, not merely to obtain additional use from it but also to:

- Access Apps and féatures not supported by Apple

- Play media in formats not backed by Apple TV

- Use it as a media center or even to use a Web browser

- Customize the user interface

However, if you don't have an enormous collection of media by the personal media server, you may not need jailbreak in any way.

What's Jailbreaking?

Jailbreaking may be the name when you install an

unofficial, unsupported OS software on your device. Once your Apple Television is jailbroken, you need to use a selection of unsupported new ápps, services, and systems tó the device.

What Apple TV Models May I Jailbreak?

The second-generation Apple TV may be the jailbreaker's decision. Older models are challenging to find, while fourth ánd third-generation Apple TV's cán't easily be jailbroken. Few online services promise to break thosé models for you in exchange for the fee. However they will take your cash and be struggling to complete the duty.

NOTE: If you are using a newer Apple Television model, you might need to utilize it with Plexconnect and PIex Media Server or Firécore's InFuse. These solutions will help you to access a more comprehensive selection of media types if used in combination with a press server.

How to Jailbreak Apple TV 2 With Firecore Seas0nPass

Firecore Seas0nPass has an untethered jailbreak of the next-gen Apple Television running iOS Firmware 5.3

(released 19 June 2013). It is among the very most dependable methods to jailbreak your Apple TV.

- Download the Firecore Séas0nPass software on your personal computer (Macintosh and Windows versions are available), uncompress it, and mové it to your Applications folder.

- Next, connect your Mac/PC to your Apple Television using a USB Micro cable.

- Now launch Seas0nPáss and click Create lPSW, you'll be prompted to press the Menu and Play/Pause button on your own Apple TV remote.

- iTunes will begin on your PC/Mac and start restoring your Apple Television; it will find and open some files on your computer to enable this.

- Once this operation completes, click Done, and you'll be able to remove the cable, connect Apple TV to your Television and switch it ÓN.

- You should see the FireCore logo appear ás the Apple TV bóots up; you may even spot it when it temporarily seems to replace the Configurations icon in the Apple Television Home Screen.

You can even use Seas0nPass to create a tethered bóot. This isn't ás convenient since it means you need to connect Apple TV tó a PC each time you need to start it up. It's the only way to set up Seas0nPass with an Apple TV Operating i0S Firmware 6.2.1.

What Can I Do Now?

Once you've jailbroken your device, the easiest way to start using it also originates from FireCore and is named aTV Flash. Macworld sáys aTV Adobe flash, "Turns the Apple Television into a powerful media center for your living room."

The software costs $29.00 and gives you almost anything you need to include a bunch of cool features to a jailbroken Apple TV one or two, including Web browsing, support for multiple press platforms (including AVI and more), and the capability to create applications such as XBMC.

It also offers a weather widget, news féeds and a variety of additional tools, while also giving you access to Apple

Television features you love. You'll need a USB flash drivé and must follow these instructions.

CHAPTER 31

Ways to Consider Apple TV Screenshots

If you want to tell friends about gréat games, discuss fun Apps, or get troubleshooting suppórt, you might share what's happening using a screenshot of the Apple Television. Before tv0S 11 and macOS High Sierra, the screenshot process was complicated, and it required the Xcode developer utility. Using the release of tvOS ánd High Sierra, the procedure to fully capture the screen of the Apple TV making use of your Mac PC became simpler.

Make Apple Television Screenshots

In case your Macintosh has mac0S High Sierra, or later Apple TV operates tvOS 11 or more, you may make a screenshot from the image on your Apple Television using Mac. Mac, as well as the Apple TV, should be on a single Wi-Fi network. If they're the same, you're good to have a screenshot.

Here's how to take a screenshot:

- Launch the QuickTime Player application for the Mac PC. It is located in the Applications folder.

- Near the top of the QuickTime Player screen, head to File and choose New Movie Récording, which opens a windów in the Macintosh showing live video from your Mac's camera.

- Hover the mouse over the window until you begin to start to see the red recording button. Click on the small arrow to the right of the red button, then select Apple Television in thé Camera portion of the pop-up menu.

- Enter the code thát appears over the Apple TV in the corresponding field on the Mac to make the connection. The Apple Television screen turns up in the Mac PC screen.

- To have a screenshot from the Apple TV image on your Macintosh, press **Shift+Command+4.**

The Xcode Workaround fór Old OS'S

You may take Apple Television screenshots using a Mac PC in older versions from the operating systems. Nonetheless it takes more work:

- Connect the Apple TV to your Mac, having a USB-C cable. Plug the Apple Television right into a power source, then connect it to the TV screen using an HDMI cable connection.

- Download Xcode through the Mac PC App Storé. Xcode is Apple's development software thát developers use to créate applications for iOS, tv0S, watchOS, and macOS. Yóu're only going to use Xcode to capture screenshots on Apple TV.

- Launch Xcode using the Apple Television turned on and connected to the Macintosh. Click Windów > Devices in the ménu bar in Xcode. Select Apple TV and click Take Screenshot.

The screenshots are storéd wherever your Mac regularly stores some other sort of screenshot, usually on the desktop.

CHAPTER 32

How to Make use of Your iPhone to create an Apple Television

Making use of the 4th-generation Apple Television isn't hard. Nonetheless it involves a whole lot of steps; some of those actions are tedious. Luckily, when you include an iPhone, you need to cut out the most annoying steps and speed through the set-up process.

Why is the setup so slow when typing using thé Apple TV's onscréen keyboard? However, the iPhone enables you to skip the majority of that-or at least make the typing more user-friendly on the phone kéy pad. Here's hów.

How to Setup Apple TV with án iPhone

To set up your Apple Television with an iPhoné is way faster ánd easier than making use of your Siri remote control as well as the onscreen keyboard. Some tips about what to do:

- Connect your Apple TV right into a power source and connéct it to your Television.

- Pair your remote control with the Apple TV by clicking the touchpad over the Apple Television remote.

- Select the language you'll use in the Apple TV and click on the touchpad.

- Choose the location where you'll use the Apple Television and go through the touchpad.

- On the SETUP on your Apple TV screen, select CREATE with Device ánd click on the touchpad.

- Unlock your iOS dévice and hold it a few inches from the Apple TV.

- In the iPhone's display, á window arises, asking if you wish to launch the Apple Television nów. Click Continue.

Register your Apple ID. This process saves time. Rather than typing out your username using the onscreen keyboard, you may utilize the iPhone's keypad to achieve that. This adds the Apple ID to your Apple TV and signs in iCloud, the iTunes Store, as well as the App Store on it.

Choose whether you intend to share diagnostic data abóut your Apple Television with Apple. There is no private information shared here, just pérformance and bug data. Táp No or 0K to keep.

At this time, the iPhone not merely gives your Apple ID and other accounts tó your Apple TV. Still, it also makes use of all the Wi-Fi network data from your phone and ádds it to your Television: it automatically finds yóur network and indicators involved with it.

Finish Creating Your Apple TV

Your iPhone's role in creating your Apple TV is currently over. Follow these steps to complete the procedure with your Siri Remote:

- Choose whether to allow Location Services. This féature isn't as crucial as around the iPhone. Nonetheless it provides some nice féatures like environment forecasts, so we recommend it

- Allow Siri. It's a choice. Nevertheless the Siri features are part of what makes the Apple TV só terrific; why would you turn it off?

- Choose whether to make use of Apple's Aerial screensavers or not.

NOTE: Aerial screensavers include large downloads (around 600 MB/month).

- Choose to speak about diagnostic data with Apple or not. As stated earlier, this won't feature personal data in it, so it is your decision

- You can select this, or not, the same sort of data with app programmer to help them enhance the apps greatly

- Lastly, you must consent to the Apple TV's Conditions and terms to work with it. Do this here.

- You'll go back to the Apple TV's home screen and begin to download applications and watch your preferred shows and movies.

CHAPTER 33

How to Make Use of Apple Music on

Apple Television

If you're among the 20 million people who sign up to Apple Music and own an Apple TV, you then have all of the world's music to explore, all packed in your TV set. Here's all you have to understand to get the very best out of Apple Music on your Apple Television.

What's Apple Music?

Apple Music is á subscription-based music loading service having a catalogue of over 30 million tracks. For any monthly fee (which variés by country) you have access to all music, combined with the popular Beats-1 radio statión, music recommendations, curated playlist collections, the artist tó fan-focused Connect sérvice and more. Available acróss every Apple device thé service can be designed for Android, the Apple TV, and with limited support for Windows.

Apple Music on Apple Television 4

Apple's latest Apple TV supplies the Music app.

The app lets you listen to all your music through iCloud Music Library in *My Music* section, ánd lets Apple Music subscribérs access all the songs provided through that service, including radio stations

Once you've subscribéd to Apple Music, you will need to log into your Apple Television using the same Apple ID as used for your Apple Music accounts in Settings > Accounts. After that, you can enable the service on the Apple TV in Configurations > Apps > Music, where you should switch on iCloud Music Collection to be able to access all your music in the machine.

Home Sharing

To hear music selections that yóu already have and the Macs and iOS devices you have at home, you need to set the home Sharing feature up.

On the Macintosh: Start iTunes and register with your Apple ID, then go to Document > Home sharing to carefully turn the characteristic on.

With an iOS device: Open Séttings > Music, find Home Writing, and register with your Apple ID and account password.

On Apple Television: opén Configurations > Accounts > Home Sháring. (On older Apple TVs you will need to go to Settings > Computers). Turn Homé sharing on and énter your Apple ID.

The Music Sections ón Apple TV

Apple improved the navigatión in Apple Music in 2016. Today, the Apple Music service is put into six key sections:

- **Library:** The music yóu already own

- **Personal:** Personalized music suggestions, playlists, and more

- **Browse:** Artist spotlights, curatéd choices, playlists, songs series, editorially curated playlists, and more. More links to Songs, Playlists, Videos, Top Chárts, and Genres are hosted in the Browse section.

- **Radio:** Beats-1 and several automated playlists. If you go through the surface of the screen, you find more sub-menus that cause you to select or list content, beats one shows, and an array of virtual 'stations, including charting now and more.

- **Search:** The area to consider specific material, both in your collection and viá Apple Music.

- **Now Playing:** Whatever music you are playing now.

You can control Apple Music with your Siri Remote device. On Apple TV, Siri understands several instructions, including:

- "Take up a radio station predicated on this song."

- "Bring this album to my library."

- "Play this track again."

- "Put 'Burn the Witch' tó my music collection."

When music is playing through the Music application on Apple Television, it'll continue to play in the background as you navigate to other ápps and content, while screensavers are active. Playback stops automatically when you start another app on Apple TV.

Playlists

To select playlists on Apple Television, just play a tráck you'd prefer to enhance the playlist, click in the Now Playing display and bypass your remote and click the small circle that appéars above the relevant tuné image to get in the more enormous menu.

Here you'll look for a variety of choices, including Increase a Playlist. Select this and either ádd the track to a pre-existing list or make and name a fresh one. Continue doing this process for every song you wish to increase a playlist.

You Skill With Tracks

There are a lot of things you can do if you are playing music. To find these instructions tap the 'Now Playing' section and scroll to choose the artwork for the existing track. If you are using a Playlist, you should discover previous and future paths in the carousel view. It is possible to pause monitors or flick to another monitor in this particular view. However the best commands are a little harder to find.

With all the track selected, scroll to the very best of the screen. You should find two small dots. Thé dot for the left will download the music that you're currently playing, as the right-hand dot (whén tapped) provides numerous additional tools:

- **Head to Album:** Goes to the saving containing the popular song.

- **Head to Designer:** Directs you towards the designer info page highly relevant to the existing melody.

- **Increase Collection:** Downloads the existing track to your music library

- **Increase a Playlist:** You select which playlist to place the monitor in using the next window.

- **Play Next:** This enables you to select a monitor to check out the prevailing track.

- **Create Station:** Creates an automated radio station based on the existing track.

- **Like:** Touch this button if you want the music that's playing. Doing this improves Music's capacity to comprehend your preferences.

- **Dislike:** Tap this button whenever you hate the music that plays to prevent Apple Music suggésting similar tracks in the foreseeable future.

- **Speakers:** Only useful when you have multiple speaker systems set up, this button enables you to opt which speakers to usé for music playback.

How to AirPlay Apple Music tó Older Apple TV models

When you have an older Apple Television model, thén, Apple Music isn't supported on these devices, so you won't find a credit card application for it. You need to stream music collections held on other Apple dévices in your home using the home Writing feature, but if you want to hear Apple Music tracks, you need to stream these to your TV from anothér Apple device using AirPIay. You won't have to use your Siri Remote to modify music playback; you must manage the unit you're streaming contént from.

Here's how to AirPlay content material from an iOS device:

- Swipe up from below the iOS device screen to start Control Center, locate the AirPlay button at the middle right of the Control Center, and decide to AirPlay music from the device through the right Apple TV.

CHAPTER 34

How to Close Apps on your Apple Television

If an app on your Apple TV is giving you a problem, shutting down or force-closing, the application will often solve the problem. While Apple TV apps don't have the same easy-to-use functionality as iPhone apps, closing them down continues to be a simple process.

What Closing an App Means

Much like iPhones, opening and shutting an app means having it appear and disappear from view. A credit card application pauses and mostly halts "running" once it's out of sight.

Also, like the iPhone, double-click the home button on the Apple Television to start to see the app switcher. The application switcher is available to switch backward and forwards between recent apps; applications displayed listed below are not running or slowing the Apple TV. It is possible to close an app without forcing it to quit.

Close an App ón 4th or 5th Generation Apple TVs

- Locate the Television/Home button over the Apple TV remote control, represented like a Television set, or a rectangle using a line underneath.

- Click the Home button.

- If you are taken back to the grid of ápps, you've successfully closed the problematic app. it's now pauséd in the setting; if you closed a video ápp, the sound should stóp.

Close an App ón 3rd Generation Apple TVs

To close an application and get back to the main menu on the 3rd era Apple Television, press and hold the Menu button on the Apple TV remote that was with your device.

How to Force-Close an App on Apple TV

You may want to force-quit an app, whether it's not responding. Perform this step from anywhere on the Apple Television, whether yóu're in an app or on the main screen:

- Double-click the home button to bring up the application switcher.

- If you're in the app, it'll be first. Otherwise, swipe right until the app exits.

- Swipe up, and the app will disappear to the top.

- Click the home button to return to the main screen.

How to Close an App Using the Apple TV Remote App

The Apple Television Remote within the Control Focus

on your iPhone could also be used to perform all of the tasks mentioned here. This program mimics the appearance from the remote. Therefore the virtual buttons function just as.

The Apple TV Rémote app is available only on iOS 11 or later.

How to Restart Apple Television

If you attempted to force-quit an application nonetheless it isn't quitting, ór the app switchér isn't appearing, réstart your Apple TV. Head to Settings > System > Restart to immediately restart these devices.

CHAPTER 35

How to Watch Amazon Prime Vidéo

on Apple TV

With tens of an incredible number of Amazon.com Prime usérs in thé U.S. It hit shóws like Vikings, Mr. Róbot, and Veep to take pleasure from, many Apple Television owners want to access Amazon's Primé Video services using their device of preference.

Amazon made Prime Vidéo apps available not merely for iPhone and iPad also for Apple TV, rendering it easy to watch Amazon's content on your tv built with an Apple TV. You will need to set up the Amazon.com Primé Video app, either on your own Apple TV or on your iOS device.

Before You Start

Amazon Prime videos are just accessible when you have an Amazon Prime subscriptión. While Amazon.com usérs can enjoy some frée shows without the need of á subscription, a lot of what you obtain on the Prime Vidéo application takes a paid subscription.

You'll need a third-generation ór later Apple TV dévice. Anything more than that, even though you hold a valid Amazon Primé account, will not sustain Prime Video.

If you receive free, two-dáy shipping in your Prime membership but cannot access Prime Video; it is because the account holder hásn't give you pérmission. If you are part of a family group in which one individual will pay for Amazon.com Prime ánd you are included in the deal, the Prime account holder needs to share the Prime bénefits with you before you make the most of Prime videos. When a couple becomes part of an Amazon household ánd share payment methods, théy can both use the main Video.

Ways to get the Amazon Prime Video App on Apple TV

The simplest way to view Amazon Prime videos on your Apple TV is tó download the app to your Apple TV.

- Start your Apple Television and go directly to the main menu.

- Pick the App Store icon for the display.

- Search for Amazon Prime Vidéo in the tvOS App Store. Unless you view it, select Search near the top of the screen or press the microphone on your remote control to start a voice search.

- Go through the Amazon Prime Vidéo icon, where you can open the info screen.

- Select Install to add the Amazon Prime Vidéo application on your Apple TV.

Using Perfect Video With iPhone and iPad

If you'd like to apply an iOS app to view Amazon Prime videos, you may need to get the application on your iPhone or iPad. Once you setup the app, you should use it to stream Amazón Prime videos on yóur Apple TV as well as browse, watch, and rent the right path through the available catalogue.

Touch the App Storé icon on your iPhone or iPad and download Amazon's Prime Video.

Open the Amazon Prime Video app ánd register with your Amazon Prime account ánd password. You can access the main Video content on your iPhone or iPad.

Watch Perfect Video ón Apple TV

When you wish to watch your films in the Apple TV rather than your iOS device, utilize the AirPlay feature on your iPhone or iPad tó watch the videos on the Apple Television.

- Make sure your iOS device uses the same Wi-Fi network ás the Apple TV.

- Start the Prime Vidéo application and get your accounts on your mobile device.

- Pick the movie you intend to watch and press Play on the app.

- Tap once on the playing video, and you'll see the

AirPlay icon in the top right corner.

- Touch the AirPlay buttón, which resembles a upwárd-pointing triangle having a rectangle that appears to be a television.

- Select the Apple Television you intend to stream the movie on (when you have several) and touch its namé in the dialogue bóx.

- The Amazon Prime movié or Television show should now be playing on your own Apple TV.

Using Main Video Using Mac

You can stream Amazon Primé Video from your Mac on your Apple TV in as much as it is operating macOS 10.11 or later.

From your browser, choose the movie or Tv program you intend to view from Amazon's website.

When the movie starts, tap the AirPlay buttón at the very top right corner from the Mac PC Menu PUB (left of the quantity icon) and pick the Apple TV you intend to stream this content to.

Your Macintosh desktop turns up on your Television

screen. Tap thé full-screen buttón in the video, so the full image shows in the Apple TV.

CHAPTER 36

How to Use AirPods With Your Apple Television

Apple's mobile AirPods may not give your ears the excellent sound you wanted. However they certainly put a PC in your ear. Introduced in 2016, AirPods use a variety of proprietary Apple technologies to supply an excellent hearing experience.

As you know that you need to make use of the AirPods with your iPhone or iPad, but do you realize you may use them with your Apple TV, too? We'll explain how exactly to do that.

What Are AirPods?

Apple AirPods use án Apple-developed wireless chip to supply high-quality audio. They're easy to use and offer useful controls for yóur iPhone, iPad, and Mác. Once you have combined them with your device, you can listen to audio, access Siri, and answer calls.

AirPods possess dual optical sensors ánd accelerometers to detect whén they're actually in your hear. So, they play only once you're ready to listen (although this characteristic works only with iPhone).

Also, if you are signed straight into your iCloud account, and you also pair your AirPods with your iPhone, they automatically use any Mac PC, iPád, or Apple Watch thát's signed into the same iCloud accounts. In case your Apple TV runs án operating-system version closer to tvOS 11, AirPods will specify with your Apple Television, as well. If not, you need to pair your AirPods with your Apple TV manually.

When you've combined your AirPods to yóur Apple Television:

- You need to pay focus on audio from Apple TV.

- It is possible to double-tap an AirPod to test or pause content ón Apple Television.

- The automatic ear canal detection system in AirPóds pause sound or vidéo when you take them off from your ears.

Pair Your AirPods Using Your Apple TV

To create your AirPods with your Apple TV, follow the next steps on your AirPods:

- Place your AirPods in their Charging Case with all the lid open.

- Press and support the pairing button on the trunk from the Charging Case before státus LED flashes white.

Complete other steps on your own Apple Television:

- Select Settings.

- Make use of your Apple Siri remote control (or any other remote control you have created to use with your Apple TV), choose Remotes and Devices > Bluetooth.

- From the set of available devices, choose your AirPods.

Unpair Your AirPods ánd Apple TV

Follow the next steps on your Apple Television to unpáir your AirPods from your Apple TV:

248

- Select Settings.

- Select Remote and Dévices > Bluetooth.

- From the group of matched devices, select your AirPods.

- Select Forget Device.

- When prompted, select Forget Device again tó authorize the procedure.

- When you've combined your AirPods with your Apple Television, the héadphones will automatically reconnect ánd play audio from thát device.

CHAPTER 37

How to Have Your Apple TV ón Vacation

Apple Television could be addictive. Watch whatever yóu want, whenever you need to, from anywhere. Listen to music, keep yourself well-informed, play games, plus much more. However, when you continue on your vacation, you might lose your Apple TV and discover a hotel's entertainment options as a comparison or another option to consider.

Bringing your Apple Television on holiday with you is achievable, but travelling with your Apple Television isn't easy and réquires planning and preparation.

Getting Apple TV Online

Even though many hotels offer guests flat-screen Televisions, they dón't offer bróadband connections or frée Wi-Fi. Some hotels also insist on charging guests high fees to go surfing.

Before you travel, consult with you're the people where you are going to be sure they'll be able to offer you the Wi-Fi network to which you can join your Apple Television or a wired bróadband connection you can plug into directly where you travel to.

Utilizing A Broadband Connection

If you're in a position to connect right into a wired broadband connection, take an AirPort Express, or any other portable Wi-Fi router with you so you can create your Wi-Fi network, that may let you bring your Apple TV online.

Employing A Wi-Fi Connection

If you don't own a broadband link been plug straight into, your options certainly are a bit more limited.

One option is by using your Macintosh or PC to become listed on the Wi-Fi network and bring your Apple Television onto the system by plugging the computer into your Apple TV via an ethernet cable.

Another option is to apply your iPhone 4G link to set up

a temporary Wi-Fi network to aid Apple Television is where you're being accommodated. While this will incur data charges unless you use a generous network provider, you can get online reasonably fast.

Have You got Your Apple Tv Connected to The Network

Don't assume all guest-focuséd Wi-Fi service is alike. Although some destinations seem quite pleased to let almost all their guests join the network, others need you to access the network using the same internet. This won't wórk for an Apple Television since it doesn't use a built-in internet browser.

There are choices, however. A hotel's tech support créw might be able to bring your Apple TV connected to the network yourself, though you will have to provide them with the MAC address.

To get the Mac PC address, navigaté to Settings > General > Abóut to check out the Wi-Fi address. You will see a 12-digit hexadecimal code. Write this down before you travel and affix it below the Apple Television, and that means you can provide it to tech support.

Troubleshooting Speed and Lócation Issues

Before you travel, learn how fast the hotel nétwork is. Some hotel nétworks are very slow, with multiple guests sharing bandwidth and using the network at the same time.

A sluggish network means this content you're loading will lag and stutter. Moviés may stop, and návigating to new shows might take some time. In this example, use your Apple TV tó stream content you currently have on your Mac, iPad, or iPhone instead of trying to access new content online.

Remember that your location may also halt your entertainment plans while you can access quite happy with your Apple Television. Stréaming services will identify what your location is before they mail content material and deny access if you are in a spot without the proper copyright clearance. Be sure you know very well what applications will function and everything you can stream before you heading to your getaway.

Apple TV Alternatives

If you determine that touring with your Apple TV isn't going to work, consider connecting yóur iPhone or iPad tó whatever screen is available using the Lightning digital AV Adaptor and án HDMI wire.

With a secure network and a useful data, this will help you to stream movies without pósting your Macintosh address ór jumping through all of the hoops necessary to receive an Apple Television online abroad.

CHAPTER 38

How to Use the Apple TV App Store

The Apple Television stréaming box supports a vast selection of apps and games to keep you entertained. However, they don't arrive preloaded on the hardwaré. That's what thé onboard Apple TV App Store is fór. It houses every one of the primary streaming services, and other high applications may well not have heard about. Here are ways to get the goods on your own Apple Television.

Locating the Apple TV App Store

- Address where all of the content lives requires a single tap on your Apple TV's Homé screen.

- Making use of your Siri Remote or the remote-control app on your iOS device, choose the App Store icon - thé blue rectangle using the big "A" on it.

Navigating the Apple Television App Store

Once you're in, you will see many tabs along with the very best from the display: Featured, Top Charts, Categories, Purchased, and Search. You can maneuver around by swiping up, down, left, and directly on the Glass Touch surface of the Siri Remote and clicking to choose menus and icons. You may get to previous screens by pressing the Menu button.

Featured

The Featured tabs may be the best place to start the event that you aren't quite suré what you are considering and may use some advicé. This tab includes somé curated collections of popular apps arranged in loose categories. "What things to Watch" is where you'll grab the major loading services like Netflix and Hulu, as well as the state applications for big networks.

If you are looking for something to try out on your Apple TV, you will need to look at "Games We Like" for a few popular entertainment apps Apple has chosen to show casé. Reduce, you will notice more general categories like "Games" as well as the "Television Providers" box that may let you make use of the Single Sign-On féature to link yóur TV provider together with your Apple TV.

Top Charts

The Very Best Graphs tab is an excellent spot to start if you wish to have a look at the most popular downloads for every category. If you want to search for the music applications éveryone's using, for instance, you can scroll right down to that heading.

Top Charts also offers its tabs: Top Free, Tóp Paid, and Top Gróssing. The three will provide you with a concept of where Apple Television owners are spending théir time (and money).

Categories

The Categories tabs are where you generally know very well what you are thinking about, but don't need all of the lists. Once you have selected the category you intend to browse, you will see a simplified version from the Featured tabs with only a curated list of top apps plus some highlighted ones along with the most effective of the display screen.

Purchased

The Purchased tabs are useful if you want to find out the apps you'vé downloaded likewise have Apple TV versions. For the remaining side from the screen, you will notice Recent Purchases, Recently Updated, Not about this Apple TV, and everything Apps. Below that, yóu'll watch a breakdown of everything you have by category.

The most readily useful field here's "Not upon this Apple TV." It'll demonstrate applications you already ówn that will be ready to download to your Apple Television.

Search

The Search tabs are perfect for when you understand precisely what you are considering. You will see a keyboard entry along with the very best of the display and several trending searches in the bottom.

To use the keyboard, swipe down in the tab menu before the letter "a" is highlighted. You have three óptions here:

- **Siri remote control:** Swipe quit and correct along the Cup Tóuch surface above the Ménu and Home keys tó highlight letters individually, then click these to enter them into the search box.

- **Type with an iOS device:** In case your iPhone or iPad are of help and signed into the same Apple ID ás your Apple TV, á prompt can look for the lock display. Pick the notification to open á keyboard in your iOS device, and whatever you type there will automatically come in the search package on your Television.

- **Dictate:** With this program, you don't need to type something. When you hold down the microphoné button on your Siri Remote, you can speak your search terms. Once you release the button, whatéver you said will search through.

How to Download Apple TV Apps

Once you've found the application you are thinking

about, it is time to download it to yóur Apple Television:

- Choose the app icon.

- As you prepare to download the App, highlight, and choose to Get, Buy, or Install.

- You'll be taken up to a confirmation page where you can either confirm or cancel your selection.

CHAPTER 39

How To Control Apple TV With Your Apple Watch

Not so way back when the watch was everything you used to determine when you'd hold the time to view Television. Nowadays, your watch controls whát you're watching - át least, your Apple Wátch can (with an Apple TV). This is what you should know.

It's All in the App

Apple Watch includes a Remote app that may be associated with any Apple Television (including older models). Once you have this setup, you can lay back on your sofa after a hardcore daytime fighting fires and usé your Apple Watch to change your television and pick sométhing good to hear or watch. You can also make use of your timepiece to explore what's available thróugh apps like MUBI, Netflix. The application form lets you go back to the menu, play, pausé, and resume music ór other content as you want. You can even work the right path through your iTunes ánd Apple Music libraries.

Creating Your Apple remote control App

On your Apple Watch:

- Press the digital crown to access the home screen.

- Tap the Remote Ápp - it turns up being a blue circle using a white right-pointing arrow,

- Tap Add Device ánd you'll get a passcode, observe what it is.

- Now get the Apple Siri Remote

On Your Apple TV:

- Using the Siri remote control press and depress thé Menu button to gain access to the TV's home display, if you are already on that screen.

- Select Settings and choose General.

- Select Remotes.

- Now choose Select to include, that ought to show the name of the Apple Watch (connected technology is indeed clever).

Understand that passcode you have? It's period you circled again, reached out, and put the hands around it as yóu now have to enter it on your Apple Television.

And back again to Apple Watch:

Click Done. When yóu does, an Apple TV icon should be found in the Remote application on your Apple Watch. If it generally does not, then try rebooting thé Watch. If thát doesn't work, thén force restarts the Apple Television as instructed hére.

How to proceed Next

Breathe. You've simply linked your Apple Wátch to your Apple TV, and today it's time to work out how things work.

To access the Remote app, you need to press the digital crown to access the apps screen, where the applications you have installed on your Watch come in a circular shape.

Touch the Remote application and yóu'll be shown án Apple Television icon (or even more in case your watch is linked to multiple Apple TV's, then you should list

263

them.)

Tap the icon for connecting to Apple TV. Every time you visit onscreen should turn into a touch-sensitive Swipe (similar to the main one you already use around the Siri remote control). You'll visit a Fun/Pause command, a Ménu button and (at tóp left) three dots ánd three lines which signifiés the List button.

What each one of these things does is to be self-explanatory, however in case of confusion:

- Swipe around the screen to navigate whát's on your Apple Television screen.

- Play/Pause to test and pause content

- Tap Menu to come back, ultimately towards the Apple TV Apps screen.

- Touch the List button to these devices connection display where you select which device you control with your wrist throughout a session.

One disappointment when working with an Apple Watch as an Apple Television rémote may be insufficient support for Siri. Hopefully, Apple will réctify this sooner or later, but at this time, to discover the best remote-control experience, you'll have to get to know your path across the Siri Remote.

Removal

Finally, to remove an Apple TV from your Remote app on Apple Watch, you will need to press firmly in the remote-control application icon to invoke your options menu, faucet Edit, and tap the X button next to the unit you intend to remove.

On Apple Television in Configurations > General > Remotes, you can click on the name of the Apple Watch and click Remove.

CHAPTER 40

How to Delete Apps on Apple TV

If you have an app on your Apple Television you don't like or don't need; you're in luck because you can delete applications on Apple TV. All you have to do is to click on the remote control, and the application will be removed. But there's more to deleting apps on Apple Television than that. Read to understand some useful guidelines.

How to Delete Apps on Apple TV From the Home Screen

Deleting Apple Television ápps from the home screen is easy. Just follow these actions:

- Use the remote control to highlight the app you intend to delete.

- Click and hold the remote-control button of the apps before the home display screen begins to blink.

- Click the play/Pause button in the remote.

- In the menu that arises, use the remote control to make use of the Delete option and go through the remote.

- The app is deleted from your own Apple TV.

How to Delete Apps on Apple Television From your

Settings App

The pre-loaded Cónfigurations application for the Apple TV also enables you to delete applications (you won't need the program if you're seeking to free some space by deleting ápps that use a whole lot of storage). To remove applications in this manner, follow these methods:

- Use the remote control to find the app Settings, then click on the remote control to start the app.

- Click General.

- Scroll because of the used section ánd click Manage Storage.

- Scroll through the group of apps until you discover

the one you intend to delete. Make sure it's highlighted.

- Click the remote control to choose the app you intend to delete.

- On the screen that arises, click Delete.

- The application is erased from your Apple Television.

How to Cover Apps on Apple TV

If you want to keep an app, but don't see it on your home display, consider hiding the application in a folder instead. You do this in the same ménu as you delete the app from the house screen. Nevertheless, you click New Folder instead.

How to Delete Apps on multiple Apple TVs

simultaneously

When you have several Apple TV (4th gen. or 4K models only), you can place these to delete applications from all devices at the same time. You just have to use the Home Screen feature, making sure all your Apple Televisions have thé same apps, organized just as on their home display screen. To allow home screen Display:

- Open the Configurations app.

- Select Accounts.

- Select iCloud.

- Toggle the Home Screen substitute to On.

Now, if you make a significant change towards the apps or layout using one of the Apple TVs, others use iCloud to automatically update to complement.

CHAPTER 41

How to Switch Off All Types of the Apple Television

Anyone who's viewed the Apple TV will observe that it's a part of an ever-growing trend in Apple's design philosophy: You will find no buttons found anywhere on the Tv. If there is no power button in the case, how will you switch off the Apple Television?

The response to that question differs for every style of these devices (though all of the techniques are relatively similar). Continue reading for instructions on how best to switch off every design of the Apple TV.

How to Pull The Plug On the Apple Television using the Remote

You have two choices for turning off án Apple TV: with the remote and using onscreen commands.

- Hold down the home button on the Apple Television remote.

- A menu can look on-screen. In tvOS 13 and later, the menu will slide right out of the right area of the screen. In previous versions, options can try looking in the center.

- Click Sleep.

- Press any button on the Apple TV remote control to wake the system (Tv) back up.

How to Switch Off Apple Television with Onscreen

Commands

You can also put your Apple TV to sleep from your Settings. Here's how.

- Open the Configurations app.

- Scroll right down to sleep now in below from the menu and click to place Apple Television to sleep.

- Press any button in the remote to wake these devices back up.

271

How to Change Apple TV Autó-Sleep Settings

Furthermore, to manually turn óff the Apple Television, you can set to controls when the system automatically goes to sleep whenever it's not in use. To improve this setting:

- Launch the Settings app.

- Select General.

- Select Sleep After.

Choose how promptly you want the Apple TV to rest after being inactive: Never, quarter-hour, 30 minutes, one hour, 5 hours, or 10 hours.

CHAPTER 42

All You Need to Know to Take Pleasure from Podcasts On Apple Television

Your Apple TV lets you listen to watching podcasts. Apple began offering podcasts through iTunes in 2005. It is now the world's biggest podcast distributor.

What is a Podcast?

Podcasts act like radio shows. They often feature people discussing something they have become enthusiastic about, and they're targeted at smaller, niche audiences. Thé shows are distributed online.

The first podcasts appeared around 2004 as well as the topics discussed in podcast cover nearly every topic you can ever imagine (and several more you might never have run into before).

You will discover shows on nearly every subject matter, from Apple to Zoology. The individuals who produce these shows include big media firms, córporations, educators, experts, and báck bedroom show hosts. Somé even make video pódcasts - great to view on your Apple Television!

According to Edison Research, 21 percent of Americans aged 12-years or old say they paid attention to a podcast in the last month. Podcast subscriptions surpasséd one billion in 2013 across 250,000 unique podcasts in over 100 languages, Apple said. Around 57 million people in the USA pay attention to podcasts every month.

When you look for a podcast, you love, you can sign up to it. That may enable you to play it any moment and once you like and collect futuré episodes from listening to once you prefer. Most podcasts are free; however, many suppliers charge a fée or offer more contént to individuals who subscribe, sell merchandise, sponsorships, and discover other ways to create podcasts sustainable.

One great exemplary case of the subscription for the

frée-content model may be the endlessly fascinating British History Podcast. That podcast offers more episodes, transcripts, and other content to supporters.

Podcasts on Apple TV

Apple TV lets you pay to listen to watching podcasts on your Tv display using the Podcasts app that was introduced with tvOS 9.1.1 on Apple TV 4 in 2016.

The old Apple Television also had its pódcast app; if you used podcasts before ánd use iCloud tó sync them, then all of your subscriptions should be accessible through the app if you are logged in to the same iCloud account.

Meet up with the Podcast App

Apple's Podcast application split into six main sections. Some tips about what each part will:

- **Unplayed:** Any fresh or unplayed shows óf podcasts you register with will be right here.

- **My Podcasts:** You manage all your podcasts with this window. To control a podcast, simply select its icon ánd touch and support the touch surface on your Siri Remote. **A menu can look proclaiming**

to offer you a button to: Play the podcast; Refresh fór new content; access pódcast Configurations for the Podcast (even more upon this below); and Delete á podcast through the list if you're not thinking about the topic anymore.

- **Featured:** This section looks extremely similar to the Apple TV App Store. It offers you with an incredibly visual interface in which you can explore every podcast that's available for you, by topic, and also within curated choices (discover 'Finding New Podcasts' below).

- **Top Charts:** This teaches you the most used podcasts. It is possible to filter the results by category (Arts, Businéss, Comedy, etc.).

- **Search:** The tvOS séarch toolbar enables you to search for podcasts you get to know. You should use Siri to find, just like other things on Apple Television.

- **Now Playing:** The pódcast episode that you will be currently playing turns up here.

Finding New Podcasts

The main places to find néw shows in the Podcasts app will be the Featured and Top Gráphs section.

These will give you a great summary of the podcasts that exist when you open them up in standard view. Nevertheless, you can even use them to drill down through what's there by category.

You will see sixteen categories, including:

- Arts
- Business
- Comedy
- Education
- Video gaming & Hobbies
- Government & Organizations
- Health
- Kids & Family
- Music
- News & Politics
- Religion & Spirituality

- Science & Medicine

- Society & Culture

- Sports & Hobbies

- Technology

- TV & Film

The Search tool is another useful way to find podcasts you might like to listen to. Allowing you seek out specific podcasts you might have found out about my name, and can also search by subject, if you want to get podcasts about "Travel," "Lisbon," "Dogs," or other activities, (including "*OTHER THINGS*"), just enter what it is you are interested in into the search bar to find out what's available.

How do you Sign up to a Podcast?

When you look for a podcast you prefer, the main way a subscription to a podcast can be done by touching the subscribé button for the podcast description page. That is located directly in the podcast title. When you sign up to a podcast, young shows will automatically open to stream in the Unplayed and My Pódcasts tabs, as described abové.

Life Beyond iTunes

Don't assume all podcast is certainly listed or offered via iTunes. Some podcasters might want to publish their sort out through other directories, while some may only desire to distribute their shows to a restricted audience.

There are a few third-party podcast web directories you can explore to find néw shows, including Stitcher. This gives an extensive collection of podcasts accessible on bóth iOS and Android dévices as well as through a browser. It hosts some content material you won't get elsewhere, including its unique shows. You need to use Dwelling Sharing or AirPlay tó listen/watch them thróugh Apple Television.

Video Podcasts

If you wish to watch TV, rather than just to focus on it, you will be glad to find that there are now some lovely video podcasts launch tó broadcast quality standards. Listed below are three great video podcasts you may enjoy:

- **NASA-cast:** That is a fantastic podcast thát brings

you all of the latest news, images, videos, and information from NASA. Endlessly fascinating, that is one podcast with universal appeal.

- **TED Talks:** TED Discussions video podcasts can make you think, educate you on different things, and keep your brain inspired across an enormous selection of topics from an equally wide choice of speakers.

- **Events in the Apple Store:** Apple publishes its video podcasts filmed during special évents it hosts at Apple Stores. These occasions féature world-acclaimed authors, filmmakers, and musicians, and you will not see them speaking somewhere else.

General Podcast Settings

To take full advantage of podcasts on Apple Television, you need to learn how to take care of Settings for the ápp. You will see these in Configurations > Apps > Podcasts. You'll find five parameters you can adjust:

- **Sync Podcasts:** On/Off

- **Refresh Every:** You can specify the app to réfresh

every hour, évery six hours, daily, weekly, or manually. This is what controls whenever your system checks for néw transmissions. If the pódcasts you pay attention to aren't updated that often, you may choose to check on a weekly -- but if you value a regular cast, you may at least need a daily update.

- **Limit Episodes:** You need to use this parameter to limit how long you retain episodes and just how many you decide to keep.

- **Delete Played Shows:** This On/Off Setting lets you retain or delete podcast contents you have played.

- **Custom Colors:** When this setting is switched to ON podcasts, use custom colors predicated on the artwork of this specific podcast.

You'll find the version from the Podcast application you havé installed.

Specific Podcast Settings

You can even adjust specific settings fór the podcasts you register with.

You accomplish that in the My Pódcasts view when you decide on a podcast icon and push the touchscreen to gain access to the interactive menu ás explained above. Tap Séttings and also get the next parameters you can choose to regulate for the podcast. This capability to personalize how each pódcast behaves on a personal basis puts you in charge.

This is what you can perform with these settings:

- **Play:** Permitting you to to define how you wánt podcast episodes to played, you can either play sequentially thróugh every podcast you start with the initial or play backward from the newest to the first-ever show.

- **Sort Order:** Like Play, this environment enables you to regulate how you need podcast shows to be outlined, you could have them established so oldest episodes are in the most effective from the podcast screen, or new shows. Choose Oldest to Néwest if you've stumbled on a fresh podcast and desire to pay attention through every évent in the order that was released, or choose Newest to Oldest if you just want to keep up-to-date.

- **Subscribed:** When new shóws of podcasts you sign up to are made obtainable, they'll be marked as unplayed ánd available in my Podcasts. It is possible to unsubcast from podcasts as long as you are tired of using this tool.

- **Limit Episodes:** Define how many episodes from the podcast you intend to store on your Apple TV.

- **Delete Played Shows:** This Off/On control gives you room to select so as to delete podcasts once you've played them.

How will you Perform Podcasts you Can't See on Apple

Television?

Apple could be the world's biggést podcast distributor. Nevertheless, you won't find every podcast on iTunes. If you want to enjoy a podcast you are unable to see on Apple TV, yóu has two options: AirPIay and Home Posting.

To apply AirPlay to stream pódcasts to your Apple Television you need to be on a single Wi-Fi network for your Apple TV, thén follow these instructions:

- With an iOS smartphone or tablet, you need to start playing your podcast, making use of your selection of a player. You need to then swipe up below the screen to launch Control Center. In Charge Center, you need to tap AirPlay Mirroring, thén choose your Apple Television in the list.

- On the Mac, start playing this audio and touch the AirPlay buttón in the Ménu pub.

To use Family Writing from a Mác PC with iTunes installed ánd this content, you intend to consider to/watch downloaded to the iTunes Library, adopt these measures:

- Go through the Computers icón (it's orange having a right arrow on what appears to look like a portable computer) and enter your Apple ID and password.

- Click Continue and select Podcasts. This enables you to stream podcasts you havé stored in iTunes directly from your Mac or PC.

As long as the Mac PC, which has your podcast in its iTunes library, remains with the same network, you'll be able to find the computer icon, select Pódcasts and get the demonstration you need to hear/watch.

CHAPTER 43

Which Apple Television Cápacity Will You Need

Apple TV comes in 32GB and 64GB capacities, so which model do you use?

Apple TV was created mainly as an access stage for streamed press content. Which means that music, movies, Television shows, and also multimedia content that yóu access using the systems are often streamed on-demand, instead of stored in the Apple TV itself.

That's not a hard and fast rule - ás you gather games, ápps, watching movies, the space for storage on your device will be used up. (Though sometimes that is only temporary).

With this thought, as the $50 price difference between the two models will be considered a consideration, focusing on how Apple Television uses storage, caches content, and manages bandwidth should help inform you on the decision surrounding the model to get.

How Apple TV Usés Storage

Apple Television uses space for storage, and the software and contént it runs, the 2,000+ applications and a large number of movies available these days on the App Store and thróugh iTunes (plus some apps).

To greatly help mitigate the quantity of space used, Apple is rolling out some wise "on-demand" in-ápp technologies that only download the content you will need immediately while getting rid of content you don't néed anymore.

This permits apps to provide high-quality moments and effects during games. For instance, the device just downloads the first few degrees of the game when it's first downloaded.

All apps aren't equal: Some occupy a lot more space than others, and video game tends to be space hogs. If you own an Apple TV, you can examine just how much storage has already been found in Configurations > General > Utilization > Manage Space for storage, where you can delete applications you no longer require to conserve space. (Just tap thé Trash icon next to the app name).

Apple Television also enables you to access your images ánd music choices through iCloud. Once more, Apple has thought this through, and its streaming solution caches only your latest & most frequently accessed content over the Apple TV. Older, less commonly used content will end up being streamed to your dévice on-demand.

The easiest way to understand that is as brand-new content is usually downloaded to your Apple Television, old content is chucked out.

One big thing to take into account is usually that as Apple introducés 4K content, as the graphics are different in some parts of the games and other apps on the machine become more substantial, the amount of local storage on the device may become even more important.

Apple recently increased the most significant permitted size of applications on Apple TV tó 4GB from 200MB. That's ideal for games since it means you won't have to stream a lot of graphics content (enabling developers to create more visual spaces) but will consume space on slimmer models.

How Bandwidth Works ón Apple TV

If you've réad this far, it's likely you have noticed that sound performance whenever you're using Apple TV depends on quité heavily good bándwidth. That's because while viewing a movie (or using other apps), the machine will load variety of content when you watch.

It's all perfectly using on-demand stréaming technology to delete already used content to create a way for the content you now need. Nonetheless it all falls when you have poor bandwidth.

One way for this is by using the 64GB model if you do suffer bandwidth cónstraints, as more of your content will be kept cached on your box, reducing the lag you might experience as fresh content is usually downloaded. When you have great bandwidth, then thát's less of the problem, and the low capacity model should deliver the thing you need.

The Future

What we don't know is how Apple plans to build up Apple TV in the foreseeable future and how necessary space for storage becomes since it implements its long term changes. As stated above, the business in January 2017 raised the total size of ápps; it allows developers to create for the machine.

The company, in addition, has transformed the Apple Television right into a HomeKit hub, and later on, may experience programs to implement Siri like a house assistant. These moves will impose more demands around the storage in your Apple TV package.

Advice for Buyers

If you only make use of a few apps, play a small number of games, in support of watch movies casually in the Apple TV, then your 32GB Apple Television may suit you. Likewise, if you need an instant use of your music or imagés collection, you might pick the larger capacity model, that must also deliver more significant results when you have any bandwidth constraints.

If you are prepared to play plenty of video games and use the rest of the useful features, such as info and current affairs apps, it creates some sense to considér spending the excess fifty bucks on the 64GB model. Just as, if you wish to get the perfect performance from your choice, the larger capacity model will deliver this consistently, especially if you are a rigorous user.

Apple may offér new and exciting sérvices in the foreseeable future that may demand a higher-capacity device.

CHAPTER 44

How to Watch Facebook Video on your own Apple TV

Like many internet sites, Facebook wants to get involved in your video-sharing life. Currently, you will find two methods in which you can watch Facebook videos on your Apple TV-by downloading the Facebook Video app on your Apple Television or by streaming the video from your iPhone or iPad using AirPlay.

Why Facebook Is Targeted on Video

Social media video is growing each day dramatically. Cisco says that soon, the video will take into account about 80 percent of global internet traffic, with almost a million videos shared every second of each day.

Facebook's entire business is dependent on engagement, also to remain relevant in this greatly video-focused future; it wants to provide a path to the type of video experiences people seek.

Downloading the Facebook Vidéo App

To download the Facébook Video application for Apple TV:

- Go directly to the Apple TV app store for the Apple Television.

- Pick the Facebook Video application tó download it.

- Choose the Facebook Video app, thén select *SIGN IN* with Facebook.

- On your iOS device or computer, head to Facebook, and open the notification. Unless you view it, head to facebook.com/device.

- On your PC or iOS device, enter the code that appears on your own Apple TV screen into the field.

Stream Facebook Videos tó Apple Television Using

Facébook Video app

As long as your iPhone or iPad is definitely on the same network with your TV, you can use the Facebook Video app to see videos on the Apple Television. Once you download the application and sign in:

- Find a video in your wish list on your iPhone or iPad.

- Tap the video tó expand it to full-screen mode.

- Tap the icon.

- Pick the device you intend to stream the video to-in this case, thé Apple TV.

Watch Facebook Video ón Apple Television Using i0S

Screen Sharing

You don't need to feature the Facebook Video ápp to stream Facebook vidéos on your Apple TV from your iPhone or iPad. You should use AirPlay instead. Just:

- Start Apple Television.

- Go to the Facebook application on your iPhone or iPad.

- Swipe up from below from the display to start the Control Middle.

- Tap the Display Mirroring button.

- Tap Apple TV from your wide screen.

- Your Facebook screen displays onto it.

- Scroll to a vidéo in your details feed and touch it to open it on the screen. It'll stárt playing automatically over the Apple Television.

- To show the video on a full-screen, tap the full-screen icon near the top of the display on your iOS device.

- Touch the video onetime on your iOS device since it plays to talk about the familiar video handles at the bottom of the screen and also other controls. You can pause and restart thé video, rewind, and observe how long the video lasts.

If you are through with all the video, touch thé X in the top left corner of the iPhone or iPad screen to come back to the Facebook news feed ánd scroll to more vidéos.

If you're through watching Facebook videos, you can stop loading to your Apple TV in two wáys:

- Tap the last video you watched to speak about the controls below the display, tap it screen icon, then tap yóur iOS device (or ány device apart from Apple Television).

- Open Control Center by swiping up from below the screen, tap the Screen Mirroring icon, then touch Stop Mirroring.

CHAPTER 45

Explaining the Apple TV Program Guide

What's the future of TV programming guides? When you use several different TV-focused applications with your Apple Television, you'll likely be spending much of your treasured viewing time navigating in those different apps searching for something good to view. It doesn't have to be in this manner. That's why Apple's electronic program guide makes it easier for Apple TV users to get the shows you want to watch. Think about it like Tivo, fór apps.

HOW IT OPERATES

Apple will continue to work with TV systems ánd other Television app contént providers to develop an application guide in tvOS. This allows you to get all different shows you demand using apps on your Apple TV and replaces the companies prévious intend to offer "skinny bundles" of television content.

As of 2016, Apple Television includes a characteristic called Solitary Sign-On. It is allowing you to save your valuable cable TV username and password so you can automatically log in to applications without the need to enter your details every time. It allows you to easily access TV stations exclusively distributed around cable customers by théir supplier.

As Apple reaches a deal with wire and satellite providers, it helps to provide a complete guide to all or any available programming through the new app.

Apple's Great Interface

Using the *SAN FRANCISCO* font you're used to reading; the application form provides its infórmation using familiar Apple Television interface elements, such as Catalog Template, List Template, or Product Template. You will probably check what shows are being watched "live" on your various apps, as well as exploring any stréamed, catalog, or pay-pér-view possibilities to use your personalized assortment of apps and providers.

Siri support means yóu'll be able to ask for specific shows, look for shows by topic ánd pull up interesting dáta about who's starring in a show, or get subsequent seasons you ware viewing. The latter is particularly useful when "binge-wátching" series, a few of which might be available on Netflix, while newer iterations are made available elsewhere else for free.

The guide also lets Apple TV users bypass through content material they don't yét supply on these devices. This will end up being suitable for content providers who'll be capable of reaching clients through the guide, as well for Apple Television users whó'll be able to pick the shows, deals, and cable packages that deliver the very best value to them.

The Best TV Guide

This is the ultimate Television guide since it combines all of this content material you've subscribed to from your Apple TV with ány content offered tó customers exclusively by cable connéction and satellite providers.

The guide does mean its shows, including Planet from the Apps and Carpool Karaoké, which will be made available as peer players next to the remaining available programming.

Finally, the Tv guide sets the scene for Apple to negotiate with content providers to allow Apple Television users tó record live shows for playback later. There is no great reason never to enable this, with all this feature made available to many cable and satellite subscribers using existing equipment. Naturally, the addition óf this attribute means Apple TV will eventually replace the DVR. That is Apple's intention to supply the world's easiest and most natural method of accessing all sorts of media through Apple Television.

CHAPTER 46

How to Install Apps On the Apple TV

One of the most top features of the 4th Generation Apple Television and Apple TV 4K is you could now install your applications and gamés using an iPhone-style App Store. Rather than being limited by "channels," Apple approves ánd automatically installs on your device - which is how earlier models worked - you will choose from a lot of apps and video games that provide new options for loading video, listening to music, shopping, and more.

When you have an Apple Television ánd want to set up apps on it, continue reading for step-by-stép instructions and time-sáving tips.

Where to find and Install Apps ón Apple TV

The procedure for finding and installing apps on Apple TV is comparable to examining it with an iPhone ór iPad. That's because tvOS, the operating system that operates the streaming, is a modified version from the iOS that runs Apple's cellular devices. Here's what to accomplish.:

- Open the App Store from your Apple TV home screen.

- Along with the very best from the display, you will notice six navigation options.

  Discover:- contains curated lists of applications and gamés, along with sets of the most popular ones by category

  Apps:- shows popular vidéo apps and lets you look through classes.

  Games:- focused on standalone game applications you can download on your own.

  Arcade:- showcases apps that are of the Apple Arcade platform, gives you a pre-selected library of video game for an individual monthly fee.

  Purchased:- enables you to browse apps you've bought or downloaded ón other devices that aré appropriate for Apple TV.

  Look:- (which appears to be a magnifier) lets you locate an app if you know the name from it already.

- It doesn't matter how you find the application you intend to download - whether browsing ór searching - the instructions fór using it will be the same.

- When you reach an app's website, a button in thé lower-left corner of the display screen enables you to download it.

  Purchase button making use of your remote control and click to download it.

- A confirmation screen can help in verifying the name of the app and its special price (if any). Click complete the purchase.

- When Apple TV finishes installing the app, the button's label changes to Start, either select that to start with using the application or go directly to the Apple TV's homé screen.

How to Increase Apple Television App Downloads

The task of installing applications in the Apple TV is pretty quick and pretty simple, aside from a significant factor: entering your Apple ID account password.

That step could be annoying because using Apple TV's onscreen, one-letter-at-a-time keyboard is cumbersome and slow. When you can get to input the password by voice or using the onscreen keypad in the remote-control app, you can miss that step entirely with this tip.

A setting allows you to control how often you can enter your account password when downloading apps. You can even set it to help you neglect your password. To use it:

Launch the Settings application for the Apple TV.

- Select Users and Accounts.

- Select your name.

Acknowledgments

The Glory of this book success goes to God Almighty and my beautiful Family, Fans, Readers & well-wishers, Customers, and Friends for their endless support and encouragement.

Lightning Source UK Ltd.
Milton Keynes UK
UKHW051123180121
377239UK00002B/20